The Turnaround Experience

Saving Troubled Companies

T. F. Schopflocher

Dedication

This book is dedicated to my two sons, Tom and Ted, who will probably choose any vocation other than business.

Acknowledgements

I should like to thank the person who innocently asked me, "What do you do when you turn around a company?" It was through my attempts to respond to this question that it occurred to me to write a book about turnarounds.

I would like to thank in particular my colleagues Michael Livingston of Action Capital Inc., Professor Peter Johnson of McGill University and my brother Peter, who with tolerance and patience read and constructively criticized the initial draft of this book.

In addition, I should like to thank Robert Cowling of the law firm Ogilvy Renault, Susan Reaman with the United States government and the J. H. Minet Company for their technical assistance.

My wife Carol and sons Tom and Ted deserve no less credit, for putting up with my endless hours in front of the computer, when I probably should have been more attentive to their needs.

Lastly, I would like to thank all my former superiors, colleagues and subordinates over the span of my working career, without whom none of my situations and experiences would have been sufficiently meaningful to permit me to write this book.

T. F. Schopflocher, January 1995.

Contents

List of Figures

Part One

Sizing Up the Situation

Spotting the Need for a Turnaround

In many respects, companies are much like humans. They are born, they grow to maturity and, after a life cycle of ups and downs, they weaken and die. Occasionally, they die prematurely. The causes of death vary, but generally fall into simple categories such as undercapitalization, insufficient diversification, poor labor relations or failure to be competitive in a demanding market place.

Very often these reason are lumped under "poor management." Management is almost always the scapegoat when a company fails, and generally with good reason. When a company is undercapitalized, it is up to management to refinance. If a company fails because the product line has reached the end of its life cycle, management should foresee the problem and diversify the product line. If a company closes because of a lengthy strike, management is to blame for having created a negative labor relations climate. And if the inability of a company to meet customers' demands for quality, delivery or price causes its demise, then the blame can be laid squarely on the shoulders of management for not having remedied the situation.

Of course, even the best of managers get caught, sometimes in situations not of their own making, and over which they have little control. New technologies emerge virtually overnight, throwing an entire product line into immediate obsolescence. Changes to government regulations covering taxes, quotas, quality standards, health standards, environmental controls and a host of other items cause shock waves to shake the foundations of entire industries.

Like humans, companies have measurable health. This health is subject to seasonal fluctuations and periodic cycling, and is affected by both internal and external forces. Internal forces might comprise human relations rifts or the loss of key personnel. But internal forces may also be less obvious and more insidious, such as a growing off-quality inventory, an increasing scrap rate, poor purchasing practices, or even employee theft or embezzlement. External forces might show up as a slowly increasing accounts receivable ledger as customers become slower to pay; higher financing costs, as banking institutions raise their prime lending rates; or perhaps a drop in sales volumes due to an economic downturn, or the appearance of an aggressive competitor.

Symptoms of poor or failing corporate health are not always immediately detected, and companies often continue to operate for months and even years before management realizes that there is a serious problem. If management is astute, many problems can be detected early and corrected before they inflict serious damage. When management waits too long to act, the damage may be irreversible and the company may become insolvent.

Verifying the health of a company takes on the same type of analysis as that of a doctor examining a patient. Routine ratios and analyses, designed to alert astute management to the condition of the company's health, should be performed periodically.

Large corporations generally possess the qualified staff to perform routine checks, and they have the means at their disposal to correct problems before they become severe. Generally speaking, the management in these large corporations is highly paid, competent and capable of understanding and quickly reacting to potential problems. And yet, we all too often hear of large and respected companies in difficulty. This has indeed happened with alarming regularity in the recent past, affecting such well known names as General Motors, IBM, Chrysler, Dominion Glass, Domtar, International Harvester, Massey Ferguson and many others, some of which no longer exist today.

At the other extreme, a small company may only be able to afford a bookkeeper, whose expertise extends only to performing a trial balance. Full statements of earnings and balance sheets may be completed by a part-time accountant, and in-depth analyses may be rarely, if ever done. Very often these smaller organizations are run by the inventor of the product line, or by an entrepreneur who had a good idea or by a person who simply inherited the family business. Depending upon the senior individual's education, background and competence, the operation of the company may be less founded on good management than on good luck. In these companies, even if the senior manager recognizes that the company faces serious problems, the company may not have the money or the staff to address them.

In between these two extremes lies the mid-sized company, with adequately competent executive talent, and whose general staff can work with outside consultants to remedy problems after they have been identified. But here too, there is a surprising lack of ability to detect serious problems, and an unwillingness to deal with them squarely. The problem could arise out of any number of reasons, but the fact remains that during hard times many companies fall into trouble, and many do not survive simply because they waited too long before taking remedial action.

Corporate problems get worse if left unattended. The problems feed on each other, affecting employee morale, company reputation, investor confidence and supplier credit terms. The credibility required to function freely in the market place begins to erode. The downward spiral often accelerates with unexpected rapidity, until the company is suddenly faced with an angry creditor.

The Turnaround Professional

The turnaround specialist is not a popular person. The position is often referred to as a "hired gun," and with good reason. A turnaround expert is hired into an organization with one objective: to clean house. Usually brought on board as a senior employee, the hired gun is given whatever title is required to confer the necessary authority to effect change. The first task of the hired gun is to assess the situation which faces the company. A rapid examination is made of the people, the culture, the structure, the policies and the financial situation, and a written report is presented to the Board of Directors or owners, indicating the assessment of the problems and outlining the proposed solutions along with a timetable. I have discovered during my career as a turnaround man that a batting average of .500 is good, and anything beyond that can be considered outstanding.

Turnaround artists are feared by company employees, because they have the authority to bring about arbitrary change. They can let employees go, hire new ones, change well entrenched policies and in general wreak havoc with sacred cows. Turnaround people are thought of synonymously with upheaval, and are sometimes given the epithet "the axe man." They are considered a necessary evil, to be brought in to rectify a particular situation, and then to be let go when the situation has been rectified. Rarely is a turnaround specialist offered a permanent position with a company after the mandate has been successfully completed. They are considered too restless, unfeeling, reactionary and unsuited for the long term management of the newly resurrected company.

The typical tenure of the turnaround expert in a given situation is short, typically one to three years, after which, if the turnaround is successful, the owner resumes control. In any case, the typical experience ends abruptly, leaving the turnaround specialist to seek another desperate situation in which to keep up a reputation for superhuman achievements. It is not a career path for everyone, but it is exciting and rewarding for those with a restless spirit and a complete disdain for job security.

Warning Signs

It is extremely difficult for the typical busy manager to see trouble coming. Day-to-day problems with suppliers, off-spec materials, late deliveries, production errors, union grievances, delinquent payers, missed deadlines and targets, and myriad other irritants often do not leave the senior managers the necessary time to sit back and evaluate the corporate climate.

Senior managers will often charge the chief accountant or chief financial officer with the responsibility to warn them when things are getting out of control. But in smaller companies, the financial personnel are so busy trying to explain monthly variances, and struggling with the apparent errors in inventory counts, not to mention the problems in getting all their ledgers to balance, that they have little time to perform the real analyses required to foresee and prevent financial difficulties. In larger corporations, the complexities generated through multi-divisional multi-national operations tend to cloud the issues sufficiently that problems are not always flagged early enough to be effectively addressed.

Perhaps the most serious obstacle to accurately predicting corporate difficulties is the fact that there are no absolute parameters to differentiate health from ill-health. Things seem to slip quickly from good to bad without being noticed, until it is too late to apply simple remedial action. To complicate matters even further, the various financial indicators vary from industry to industry, and to some extent from company to company within a given industry. Historically, it seems that drastic action after-the-fact is more prevalent than defensive action before-the-fact.

For example, the food industry might typically have an inventory turnover of fifteen to twenty times per annum, as opposed to the home appliance industry with a turnover of three to six times. But if a particular food company notices that its inventory turns are only twelve, who is to say that this figure represents a coming problem? The variance may have been caused by the introduction of a new product, and in fact the figure may indeed be perfectly normal for that particular company and its new product line.

The best method to determine whether the company is healthy or headed for trouble is to constantly monitor a series of financial and operating parameters and to graph the results, so that the senior operating and financial managers will constantly be aware of the trend of the company's health. It is not so much the absolute value of the most recent results, but the trend line which is important. If the trend is negative, then remedial action can be taken.

The concept described above is simple and elementary. However, despite the simplicity of the plan, few companies follow this procedure. By the time the senior managers realize there is a problem, it is generally too late to correct the situation without calling for outside help. Typically, it is the bank manager who alerts the company's financial officer that certain covenants are being breached, and that immediate remedial action is required, "or else."

All too often, the slope of the trend is steep. It may already be too late for the normal corrective steps, and drastic action may be needed. There are cases where companies fail quite suddenly, due to unexpected outside pressures which are unpredictable, such as sudden product obsolescence. This has happened several times in the fast-moving electronics industry when a company introduced a conceptual breakthrough, rendering conventional products obsolete. For example, the photocopier made carbon paper obsolete. The computerized word processor and the fax machine have played havoc with the traditional typewriter industry. In such cases, the turnaround might depend upon increased product innovation and development, which could involve prohibitively expensive research and testing.

Other, less dramatic events may cause sudden reversals in a company's fortunes. A large competitor might flood the media with an expensive and novel advertising campaign, effectively biting into the smaller company's market share. Or a large competitor might begin a price-cutting campaign, aimed at putting the smaller company out of business.

In addition, the normal cyclical business turndowns or periodic recessions, which occur with abysmal regularity every five to ten years, seem to catch even the most astute managers by surprise. Often caught in the middle of an extensive new product launch, or an expensive acquisition, they appear powerless to react with sufficient speed and depth to prevent financial chaos.

Some of the specific parameters which any astute manager should monitor on a continuous basis are described below. It is the performance of these parameters which will help to provide some of the early warning signals that financial problems are lurking around the corner.

Sales volumes

It should be obvious that sales volumes must be continously monitored and tracked. Comparisons must be made not only month to month, but year to year, showing this year's monthly sales against last year's, and this year's Year-to-Date against last year's Year-to-Date. Any drop in volume, either in total or by specific product line, should be questioned and analyzed.

If total demand is dropping, then two series of basic questions must be asked:

1. What is the reason for the drop in sales? Is the product line becoming obsolete, is the marketing effort as effective as it should be, or has there been a general drop in demand?
2. What remedial steps should be taken? Are product modifications required, should additional products be launched, should changes be made to the marketing strategy (i.e., advertising, distribution, merchandising, service calls and so on), or should certain product lines and projects be dropped (rationalizing), and the staff cut back (downsizing)?

Accounts receivable

One of the surest indicators of impending hard times is an increase in accounts receivable (A/R) days. This is calculated by taking the estimated annual sales figure and dividing by 365, which provides the average sales per day. By dividing the outstanding accounts receivable by the average sales per day, the result gives the number of days of sales represented by the receivables. The outstanding A/R days should be tracked weekly, and graphed.

$$\frac{\text{Annual Sales}}{365} = \text{Average Sales per Day}$$

$$\frac{\text{Outstanding Accounts Receivable}}{\text{Average Sales per Day}} = \text{Number of A/R Days}$$

Typically, in good times the A/R days might fall in the range of 30 to 45 days, depending upon the industry and the effectiveness of the credit and collections department. As economic times begin to harden, the figure may climb to 55, to 60 and even higher.

Remedial action can include tightening credit restrictions, intensifying collection procedures and offering increased discount terms. However, a word of caution is advisable when it comes to offering discount terms. When cash becomes short, it is tempting to offer better and better discounts to entice delinquent customers to pay faster. But one can end up "giving away the store." For example, if the cost of borrowing money is 8% per year, then each week costs 0.15%. If the company wishes to reduce the payment schedule by seven weeks (i.e. payment is requested in 10 days instead of the anticipated 60 days, thus saving 50 days or seven weeks), then the discount must be worth slightly more than 1% (i.e., 7 x 0.15%) in order to be enticing to the customer. In this situation, if a 2% discount were offered for early payment, it would likely be accepted, since for the customer the cost of borrowing money for this seven-week period would only be 1%. Yet, I have been in a company which offered as much as 5% in its panic to obtain much-needed cash, which virtually wiped out all the profit and some of the overhead recovery for the job. One has to strike a sensible balance between what is enticing for the customer, and what is acceptable from an operating point of view.

Labor per unit of output

In some industries, the cost of labor is a small portion of the total costs. However, in most companies, labor cost is significant and should be tracked. Depending upon the nature of the product, the measurement of labor cost as a part of output may vary. It can be measured as dollars per unit, hours per ton or any combination of parameters which make sense for the particular company. The measure should be tracked continuously. Any rise in labor content should be questioned and examined closely. An upward trend could be explained by a change in product mix, but if the upward trend is caused by a reduction of work in the shop, then action should be taken immediately to reduce the personnel levels accordingly.

This concept should also be carried to the support functions. It is reasonable to assume that such functions as research, engineering, accounting, marketing and so on must justify their costs based upon the ability of the company to pay. Total payroll should also be continuously tracked, and if a downturn in revenues can no longer justify the salaried overheads, then action should be initiated aimed at reducing personnel wherever possible.

Inventory turns

One of the important indicators that is often neglected is inventory turns. Simply stated, this can be a measure of how much slow-moving or dead stock is building up in the warehouse. For companies which produce a standard product for inventory to be sold later, a slowdown in general sales levels can mean a build-up of inventories whose cost to manufacture may not be recovered for several years.

Inventories are costed at the cost-of-goods-sold level (the sum of direct labor, raw materials and manufacturing overheads), and do not include selling, financial, research or administrative costs or profits. Therefore, inventory turns are calculated as the estimated annual cost-of-goods-sold divided by the estimated average inventory value. The absolute numbers vary significantly by industry and even by company within industries, so that the real value of tracking the inventory turns is to monitor the trend for the individual company.

A steady lowering of inventory turns can signal serious problems for the company cash flow, and should be addressed immediately. Production may have to be curtailed, layoffs may be required, and raw materials purchases or delivery schedules may have to be reduced.

Interpreting inventory turns can be complicated by a cyclical product demand. To cite an extreme case, I have an acquaintance who operates a company which manufactures specialty products, which are sold mainly for the Christmas season. All year long, the company builds up inventory until the Christmas season, during which time virtually all the inventory is sold. The cash required to build up this essentially non-moving inventory is enormous, and requires a certain leap of faith on the part of the bank manager. The fear is that public tastes will change, and the company will not clear out the inventory build-up, and will be left with mountains of obsolete stock. Fortunately, most companies do not have these problems.

Bank indebtedness

The short term bank loan, or line of credit, is the buffer which allows a company to survive the periodic cash shortfalls which are normal in any business. The company's bank will fix a maximum not-to-exceed value for the line of credit, and this line of credit is secured by fixed assets. The value at any instant in time is determined by a pre-agreed portion of the value of inventories (depending upon the nature of the business, often up to 50% of finished goods and up to 35% of work-in-process) and 75% of the active receivables below 90 days. In Canada, this line of credit can be kept open all year around, and the company can draw upon it at all times, as long as the pre-set limit is not exceeded.

In times of difficulty, as the active receivables grow and the inventories of unsold stock invariably grow, the line of credit becomes utilized to its maximum at all times. The astute senior manager will monitor the bank indebtedness continuously, and will recognize that as the used line of credit approaches the maximum allowable, the company is limiting its ability to absorb the normal cyclical peak cash demands which are a normal part of doing business.

Cash flow forecasts

Cash flow forecasting involves, to some extent, predicting the unknown, and is therefore an unpopular activity. The responsibility for predicting cash flow is usually entrusted to the chief financial officer or chief accountant, and in most companies cash flow forecasting is simply ignored. It is, however, one of the more important tools at the disposal of senior management, to predict and avert financial difficulties.

In truth, much of the cash flow forecast for any company is known with a good deal of certainty. Wages and salaries can be predicted with some accuracy. Invoices for services and periodic obligations such as insurance premiums and business taxes are known with reasonable accuracy. Receivables can be predicted quite closely if the customers are known, and payables (including cheques in the float, e.g. sent but not cashed) are predictable with great accuracy, since they are under the direct control of the accounting department. Figure 13 (see page 97) shows a typical weekly cash flow forecasting format.

The real difficulty lies with the forecasting of coming sales. It is precisely here that predictions can fall apart and the root cause of future financial problems be found. The forecast of sales should not be a simple copy of what was budgeted months before. It should be a realistic attempt to describe what the sales will really be, and the forecast should be worked out with the sales manager. Understandably, the projected sales may have little to do with the original budgets.

In addition, the down-side sales levels should also be targeted, and a "worst case" cash flow projection should accompany the "expected case" projections. The "worst case" may be an educated guess, taking into account historical data of previous sales slumps, the economic climate, the strength of the competition, changes in public tastes or any other factors that are known to have a potential negative effect on sales levels.

The cash flow projections should be performed periodically, preferably on a rolling two-week basis, and should show projections as far into the future as six months. In this way, every two weeks the senior manager will have the opportunity to see a revised and updated forecast of the company's projected cash position, and can take timely action if the projections so indicate.

The difficulty for the senior manager is to decide just how large the cash buffer should be, and how long the down-turn will last. There are no exact answers to these questions, and in recent times even such giants as IBM and General Motors have been delinquent in reading the warning signs, much to the chagrin of their former chief executive officers!

Taking action

If the warning signs described above begin to suggest that the company is headed for trouble, there are at least four important steps that should be taken.

1. The senior manager should ensure that the periodic financial and operating information generated by the sales, production and accounting departments is both accurate and timely. There is nothing more frustrating for a company president than trying to determine the extent of the problem, or determining a realistic course of action, based upon information which is out of date. Financial statements must be timely, and preferably should be issued within four working days after the end of each financial period. It is often useful to have interim statements issued, if the extra burden on the accounting department can be absorbed.

2. Begin to extend the accounts payable (A/P). Typically, the accounting department will watch the accounts receivable climb steadily up to 60 days and more, but will still pay its invoices inside 30 days, usually out of force of habit. Extending the A/P can have serious repercussions with suppliers, and must be done with care. Generally, it is best to speak with each supplier in advance. Ideally, the A/P days and the A/R days should be the same; when the A/R days exceed the A/P days, the cash shortfall is being financed through the bank line of credit which may already be nearing its maximum allowable.

3. The senior manager must begin to take a more active role in limiting unnecessary expenditures. It is a serious decision to determine which expenditures are to become "unnecessary," and almost any decision will be unpopular with some of the employees. Typically, company social functions are the first casualties in an austerity campaign. Expenditures on new furniture, office renovations, employee expense accounts, office supplies and other "frivolities" are usually next, followed by a hiring freeze on all new positions, part-time employees and finally on replacement employees.

The real difficulty for the senior manager is to cut sacred cows; building expansions, product development projects, foreign market penetration projects, staff training programs and especially those projects where money has already been spent. Unless the company truly cannot afford to cut a project without seriously jeopardizing the company's future, any and all expenses must come under serious scrutiny. If the early warning signs are strongly indicative of impending financial difficulties, the senior manager must be strong enough to overcome the inevitable objections of his staff to any program cuts.

How much to cut will depend largely upon the cash flow forecasts, which, depending upon their accuracy, will indicate the potential extent of the coming cash shortage. Business is not an exact science, and judgement, experience and luck all play an important role in the outcome.

4. It is strongly recommended that the senior manager advise the company's bank manager of the coming difficulties, and to apprise the bank manager of the action steps being taken to ride out the coming storm. Bank managers are very friendly when a company does not need them. But they become notoriously unfriendly and unreceptive when a company is in financial difficulty. The best way to avoid an unpleasant confrontation with potentially catastrophic consequences is to make sure the bank manager is aware of the problem, and to ensure that he or she is comfortable with the plan of action. Bank managers do not want to operate troubled companies, and will not normally interfere with day-to-day operating

decisions, unless circumstances offer no alternative. As long as the situation is under control and is being properly addressed, the typical bank manager will permit the company management to manage without interfering.

There are no guarantees that the action steps will stave off a serious financial crunch. All too often, economic downturns catch company managers by surprise, totally unprepared for the drastic nature of the steps which must follow. Younger managers who have not lived through a serious recession sometimes cannot understand the need to take severe and often distasteful action to save the company. This book deals mainly with this latter aspect of the problem.

Providing the Initial Shot of Adrenalin

A company in need of a turnaround is invariably cash-poor. In the extreme case, payables have been extended to the breaking point, and most if not all suppliers have given notice that all purchases will be on a COD basis. Meeting payroll is a weekly or bi-weekly nightmare, and the line of credit is at its maximum. The president will have been given ample warning by the lending institution that remedial action had better be taken immediately.

In cases where the situation has not reached this extreme condition, there will be sufficient time to perform an analysis without embarking on a crash program. But even in these cases, the turnaround specialist must possess a keen sense of urgency and must prepare the analysis together with the plan of action within four weeks or less. By the time a turnaround person has been called in, there is little time for analysis. The typical situation can be described as a race between the turnaround specialist and the bank manager, to see whether the turnaround person can generate the much needed cash before the bank manager decides to "pull the plug."

It is generally considered a wise practice to begin by paying a visit to the company's bank manager. The objective of this visit is to reassure the bank manager that the company has officially recognized that it is in difficulty, and that it is now prepared to take whatever drastic steps that may be required to put it back on track. Bank managers do not like surprises, but this news may come as a pleasant surprise. The bank manager will undoubtedly want to be informed of the plans to turn the company around, and to be given a reasonably detailed pro-forma financial portrait of how the turnaround will transpire. He or she will definitely want to be kept aware of the periodic progress against the established targets.

There is a rule of thumb that says one never gives a bank manager more information than is needed. There is good reason for this thinking. Bank managers do not wish to run your company. Nor do they wish to make management decisions for your company. But they do wish to be informed, and to avoid nasty surprises. The turnaround expert must attempt to gain credibility and to develop a professional relationship with the bank manager, and to feed the manager periodic information demonstrating progress toward a turnaround.

If the company is indeed in extreme financial difficulty, then the first priority is to find cash in order that operations can continue. This simply means that the job of the turnaround person will be that much more hectic while attempting to figure out what is wrong and what to do about it. There are several places which often prove to be sources of cash.

Extend Accounts Payable

The simplest way to finance any operation would be to avoid paying the bills. That way, there would be no cash outflow. Of course, this is not feasible with payroll obligations, or management would find itself without personnel to operate the company. Neither is it feasible with essential services such as the telephone. The phone utility would simply cut off the phone system, and the company would become inoperable. It is traditionally the suppliers of competitive services, raw materials and supplies who must bear the brunt of the practice of extended payment. The objective is to identify suitable services and suppliers, and extend their payment schedules as far as possible.

Raw materials usually comprise a very significant portion of cash outflow, and the raw materials suppliers should be among the first targets for extension of payments. Very often the suppliers are surprisingly understanding when approached properly and told of the company's problems. Particularly if they are made to understand that the situation is temporary, and that there are major efforts underway to turn the situation around. Of course, there are those cases where the supplier's receivables are collected by a factor, who will simply not permit any extension. Some suppliers represent monopolies in the company's geographical area, and will simply threaten to cut off supply if payments are extended beyond a specified time limit. These are, fortunately, isolated cases.

Suppliers of office supplies, computer paper, office equipment rental, legal advice, and repair and maintenance contractors must also be considered for the practice of extended payment schedules. Unfortunately, being relatively small suppliers, the courtesy of an explanatory phone call is all too often neglected. When the supplier refuses to deliver any more goods until payment is made, the company may simply search out another supplier and ring up another series of invoices for extended payment. Suppliers, it seems, do not talk to each other, perhaps due to competitive secrecy, so companies can often switch to a second and even a third supplier, if necessary. This is not a recommended practice, and can result in contributing to the ultimate insolvency of the small supplier.

Then there are the services, which must also be considered for extended payment, such as key-employee life insurance premiums, group health premiums, fire and theft premiums, business interruption premiums and so on. It would be poor business practice to extend payments without first advising the suppliers, and often an explanatory phone call to a senior person in the supplier company will fall upon receptive and understanding ears. If the supplier company proves unreceptive, then extending the payment of outstanding invoices may result in the discontinuance of service. That is a risk one has to take. But it may be better to continue to operate without insurance, and take the chance, than to head into certain bankruptcy.

I am not advocating unethical business behavior. I am merely pointing out that the extension of payables is one way to temporarily finance a company's cash shortfall. The degree of extension of payment schedules varies with each case, but can typically become as much as 90 to 120 days. If most of the suppliers have already placed the ailing company on a COD basis, then this window may already be closed.

Depending upon the size of the supplier, and the company's historical relationship with the supplier, payables may be stretched without undue difficulty. However, in some cases the extension of payables, if stretched too far, may suddenly result in a demand for COD or, even worse, CBD (Cash Before Delivery). These undesireable situations defeat the purpose of extending payables, except inasmuch as prior invoices may remain temporarily unpaid. Many companies will insist that small payments be made regularly towards outstanding invoices. It is necessary to negotiate the smallest payments possible.

The damage to the company's reputation and the willingness of the suppliers to resume normal relations with the offending company are questions to be taken into account when making the decision to extend the payment schedule. At best, extending payables is to be considered a short-term course of action, and the situation should be normalized as quickly as possible.

Collect Outstanding Receivables

It would amaze people that even in companies which are strapped for cash, there are often outstanding receivables which go uncollected for extended periods. Perhaps there is something about asking for money which offends people in our culture, but one of the first places to look for available cash is inside the Accounts Receivable ledgers.

One company for which I did some work had sales of less than $5 million annually, and was extremely short of cash. So short, in fact, that there was some question of the company's ability to survive past the end of the month. The company had a controller at the plant level, and a senior financial officer at the holding company level, each of whom was acutely aware of the financial situation of the company. Just as things were looking desperate, a large customer called the president and asked him when his company was going to invoice its last shipment. Awestruck, the president sat down and closely examined the receivables, to discover to his amazement that there were over $100 000 of uncollected receivables available for the asking.

This is not an unusual or isolated incident. Despite the watchful eye of several layers of financial expertise, it should not surprise a turnaround person that there are receivables past due. In part, this is caused by customers who are extending their payables, in much the same way as the turnaround expert will attempt to extend the company's. These will prove difficult to collect. But in part, this situation is caused by negligence or by a lack of available staff to do collections.

In a turnaround situation, the collection function takes on new relevance. Companies which never had to concern themselves with carrying out careful credit checks or dispatching sales representatives or clerks to collect cheques suddenly recognize the merit of dedicating a person to the function of collections, if only for the duration of the turnaround.

Not just anyone is qualified to do collections. The person charged with this responsibility must have considerable tact when dealing with harried payables clerks at the other end. But they must also have the persuasiveness and the authoritative manner to impart the seriousness of the request for payment. Nice people are pleasant to talk to on the phone, but they do not collect much money. Curt people, on the other hand, tend to annoy the recipient of the call and harden his or her resolve to resist the demand for payment. The ideal collections person has a blend of qualities which optimize the ability to collect money. It is probably safe to say that the ideal collections clerk will cause from 2% to 5% of the customers to actively complain about the abuse of their payables clerks. Less than that suggests that the collections clerk is being too lenient; more than that and the company is risking damage to its customer relations.

The collections clerk should be trained to call customers within several days after shipment of the goods, and request early payment. If the company has been on good business terms with its customers, there is sometimes a chance that some larger customers will pay a portion of the invoice in less than the standard 30 days. Sometimes, if cash is required immediately, it is possible to negotiate terms such as 3% net 10 days, and I have had to offer as much as 5% net 10 days just to receive some much needed cash.

In order to astutely manage the company's cash, it is neccessary that the payables and the receivables be properly aged. With today's readily available computer technology and financial software, it is assumed that the company possesses the required data, which can be processed, updated and printed out as required for the use of management and the collections clerk. If such time-based information is not readily available, the chances of success in collecting receivables and managing payables are minimal.

Control Outgoing Requisitions

Purchasing agents and buyers are taught to follow certain well conceived rules in order to save companies money. Always ask for at least three quotations. Wherever possible buy in bulk to save money, and ask the supplier to maintain the inventory. Negotiate blanket orders, and so on. These rules stand companies in good stead during normal times, and can save a great deal of money. In a large corporation, an annual savings of one-half-of-one-percent in raw materials can represent an enormous amount.

The turnaround situation changes the rules. There simply isn't the cash to buy in bulk, no matter how great the unit cost savings might be. There isn't the cash to buy a four weeks' supply, even if a one week's supply raises the unit cost. In a turnaround situation, the lack of cash dominates all thinking and all actions. Sensible purchasing concepts become subordinate to practical reality.

In a small to medium sized company, I have found it to be extremely wise for the turnaround person to set up a procedure whereby each and every purchase requisition must be authorised and signed by him or her before it can be processed. In this way, there can be no surprises. The turnaround expert can determine what quantity of materials or supplies the company can afford, and can ensure that these minimum quantities are adhered to. If the order in the shop only requires four transformers, then four are ordered, not six, even though more transformers may possibly be required next month, and even though an order of six would reduce the unit cost by 5%.

In a small to medium sized company, the turnaround person can insist upon signing all purchase requisitions, from the large raw materials items which may cost several thousands of dollars, down to the nitty gritty items such as soaps and mops. In one instance I can still picture the irate union steward who stormed into my office red faced, and blustered, "You and your damned cost savings! There's not a stitch of toilet paper in the whole company!" Sometimes you can shave it too close.

In a larger company, it becomes impractical to scrutinize each purchase requisition, and the job will have to be delegated to key trusted individuals. But the objective is the same: purchase only what is absolutely required, and purchase only a one (or two) week supply where delivery delays permit. In the long run, this is a costly practice. But in the short run, it may save the company from insolvency.

Control Outgoing Cheques

In a small to medium sized companies, it would be wise for the turnaround person to add his or her name to the cheque signing procedure, and to advise the company's bank that this name must appear on the cheques. In fact, this is just a formality. I have seen cheques passed with only one signature where two were required; with the wrong signature; and unfortunately with forged signatures. The procedure, though well-meaning, is simply not enforcible in many banking institutions. Nonetheless, the fact that the person in charge of the turnaround must sign all cheques keeps him or her abreast of all outgoing funds, and gives some control over which cheques are paid and when they are paid.

In a larger company, this procedure can become cumbersome and impractical. But a procedure can be instituted whereby the turnaround person must sign all cheques over a certain specified amount. This amount can vary, depending upon whether the cheque is for a service, for supplies or for raw materials.

Be Wary of Extending Credit

The temptation to acquire new customers can be overwhelming to a company short of cash. Any means to increase sales is looked upon as a means to solve the company's ills. But the chances are that if times are tough for one company, they will be at least moderately difficult for many others as well. Not all potential customers will be able to pay quickly, and an indiscriminate choice of new sales targets can lead to disaster, especially during a turnaround. Nothing could be worse for the cash-poor company than to purchase raw materials, pay labor to produce a product and ship the product, only to discover to its chagrin that the brand new customer cannot or will not pay its bills on time. The credit function of the credit and collections clerk is extremely important to the company in trouble, and must be rigorously exercised. A short phone call to a credit service bureau is well worth the small cost.

Sell-off Unused Inventories

Inventories are a jungle, full of lions, tigers and alligators. They tend to be the general receptacle for all the production department's mistakes, for the sales department's errors in judgment and for the finance department's need to balance the books. They invariably contain off-standard product and obsolete stock, and they are probably valued at close to full cost irrespective of how many years they have been in the warehouse. When inventories become fixed assets, it spells trouble.

One's first impulse is to simply clean house and start all over again with a clean slate. But it quickly becomes apparent that if, indeed, some or all of the off-standard or obsolete inventories are on the books at full (or in fact any) value, the shock to the balance sheet of writing off all the unusable stock may be too great for a financially troubled company to bear.

In one company that I was helping out, some of the inventory had been in the warehouse for six years without moving, and the books still showed this stock at full original value. The auditors had just come and gone, but there was no change to the inventory values. Although the owners of the company were delighted with the status quo, I knew that this state of affairs was going to cause problems some day farther down the road.

The immediate question is whether any of this inventory can be sold at any price. The dilemma is that if the inventory is sold at below book value, the company will show a worse loss than if the inventories had remained in the warehouse.

But if the inventory can be sold at even a fraction of its book value, the resulting sale will bring in much needed cash that otherwise might be forever tied up in inventory.

Off-standard inventory generally means that the printed colors were not exactly what the customer had ordered, or the size of the sheets were cut one-half inch too short, or that, for some reason associated with quality, the original customer had refused the shipment. The production lot was not considered scrap at the time of production, and was probably placed in inventory in case the customer could be persuaded to accept the product at a later date. If the inventory is indelibly marked with the original customer's logo, and the customer doesn't want to accept it even at a reduced price, then the company may indeed be stuck with it. But if the inventory is not identified to a particular customer, it may well be of interest to other potential customers or jobbers, if the price is right. Even a scrap dealer may be interested, if the inventory contains materials that could be sold on the commodities market.

Obsolete inventories are usually the result of over-production which was never sold, or the result of over-buying of colors or styles which went out of fashion. There may be nothing fundamentally wrong with the inventory except that it won't sell in the usual market place. Again, jobbers and scrap dealers may be interested, and there may even be an opportunity to sell in bulk to an off-shore country or jobber, who may not be so fussy about color and style if the price is right.

There are never any guarantees that excess inventories can be sold, even at greatly reduced prices. In addition, the shock to the financial statements, even if one is successful in selling inventory at below book value, can be frightening at the end of the fiscal period. But when a company is fighting for its life in a turnaround situation, any chance to obtain immediate cash may override future considerations.

Forestall Interest Payments

Sometimes lenders, both private and institutional, will agree to capitalize interest payments in order to ease the financial burden for an ailing company. It is up to the turnaround person to attempt to negotiate such arrangements. The burden of debt is effectively increased, because when interest payments resume they are calculated on a larger base; but the immediate effect of such a move is to reduce the immediate cash outlay requirement.

Dispose of Assets

Occasionally, the company may be sitting on a veritable gold mine without realizing it. For example, the company may own one or more buildings, and in very fortunate cases does not even have a mortgage. The objective here would be to sell the building, and then lease it back under a long-term leasing arrangement. I have seen this done very successfully, and it can be an excellent source of cash. Unfortunately, selling buildings is not generally done quickly, and the company may find it difficult to quickly finalize what it considers to be a fair deal. Furthermore, in times of recession, the value of the property may have dropped considerably below what the owners believe is reasonable. In one company which I was helping, the president and owner negotiated the sale-leaseback for more cash than the building was worth, but agreed to a higher than normal interest rate to compensate for the high purchase cost. And of course, one can second and third mortgage a property to obtain cash, with the understanding that these mortgages will carry a heavy price tag for many years. But in stormy times, any port appears inviting.

Another area to look at is the company fleet. If a company is large enough to operate a fleet of trucks, cars or lift trucks, sometimes these fleets are owned by the company. Depending upon the age and condition of the vehicles, this fleet can be sold and leased back over a period of several years. The sale of the fleet could bring in much needed cash.

Very often a company will have old unused machinery and equipment lying in a corner of a warehouse which might be useful to a third world country. This is becoming less attractive today, as third world countries are increasingly eligible to receive excellent financing grants to purchase modern machinery from industrialized nations. Equipment brokers do not pay much for used machinery. But every now and then, a company may have a specialized piece of equipment which it can part with, which may yield a surprisingly large amount of cash. The possibility should not be overlooked.

Lay-off Personnel

Reducing management and clerical staff and labor is one of the more difficult tasks that a manager will ever have to perform. When I first got into the turnaround business, invariably I would have to reduce the number of people in the workforce and then follow up with a reduction to the corporate structure. At first, I would lie awake nights thinking about the terrible thing I had done to the individuals who had lost their jobs. What were they going to say to their wives and children? How would they maintain their self-esteem, and how would they feed their families? As time went on, I never really got used to the idea of laying workers off, or firing management or clerical personnel, but I realized that the company was fighting for its life, and if letting 10% of the people go meant saving the jobs of the other 90%, then all the pain made sense.

A company does not normally "lay off" management and clerical staff. If a troubled company downsizes its staff, this move can be considered quite permanent, and those let go should normally not await re-hiring within a foreseeable time frame. When letting go management or clerical personnel, the event is accompanied by a cheque for termination pay. This cheque can be quite sizeable, particularly if the person is a senior manager, because the laws against termination without just cause have become stringent in North America. Thus, the act of terminating a manager or clerk can be expensive, and is not considered part of a "quick fix" to save expenses.

Hourly-paid labor, on the other hand, is treated more as a commodity, to be hired and laid off as the economy dictates. An hourly-paid laborer can be laid off today and re-hired six weeks from now, with only one week's pay as notice. Hourly-paid personnel may be unionized or non-unionized. Union contracts deal with layoffs through very clearly defined rules. The last in shall be the first out, and there is a specified period of notice before a layoff can go into effect. Then the seemingly interminable "bumping" begins, bringing with it its usual disruption and requirement for training and re-classification. The labor contract will also clearly specify how long the layoff will be considered a temporary layoff, before it is considered a permanent layoff requiring the payment of termination benefits.

Although the rules dealing with non-unionized workers are less well defined and less rigid, many employers like to treat the non-unionized employees at least as well if not better than their unionized counterparts, in order to eliminate the possibility of angering them sufficiently to become unionized.

How does one know that a layoff is warranted? There are at least four ways. The first is to compare the "paid direct labor hours per unit of output" for each of the past five years, and determine a trend. An example of a comparison of paid direct labor hours per unit of output might be as follows:

July 1993: Paid direct labor hours   = 8 640
              Units Produced   = 1 262

$$\text{Paid direct labor hours per unit produced} = \frac{8\,640}{1\,262} = 6.85$$

July 1994: Paid direct labor hours   = 9 470
              Units produced   = 1 045

$$\text{Paid direct labor hours per unit produced} = \frac{9\,470}{1\,045} = 9.06$$

In this example, the production efficiency is less efficient by (9.06 - 6.85)/ 6.85 or one third. This assumes there were no appreciable product-mix changes and that the comparison is fair. If the company is truly in difficulty, then the chances are that the current paid direct labor hours per unit of output are significantly higher than they were when the company was profitable. This assumes, of course that the product and/or the product mix has remained unchanged during the five year period.

If, indeed, the product or the product mix has changed over the period of measurement, then one must compare the "standard direct labor hours per unit of output" against the actual paid hours. This assumes that the company has some knowledge of the "standard" hours that it takes to produce a particular end-product. Not all companies do, particularly the smaller ones. An example of this comparison follows.

August 1993: Standard hours to produce

one unit	= 17.6
Units produced	= 765
Total standard hours = 765 x 17.6	= 13 464
Total hours actually paid	= 16882

$$\text{Plant efficiency} = \frac{13\,464}{16\,882} = 80\%$$

August 1994: Standard hours to produce

one unit	= 16.2
Units produced	= 702
Total standard hours = 702 x 16.2	= 11 372
Total hours actually paid	= 18 044
Plant efficiency	= 63%

In the above example, the plant efficiency fell from 80% to 63% inside one year. Was this drop due to the learning curve to manufacture a new product? Or was it due to poor labor control? It will be the job of the turnaround person to identify the reasons and to determine a suitable course of action.

If the second method is not available, then very often the practised eye will quickly determine whether there are too many employees on the floor by simply taking an extended walk through the shop. This method is, to be sure, very subjective and is not entirely accurate. But someone who has a good appreciation of an industrial shop floor, or who has worked in the troubled company's particular industry for several years, can rapidly tell whether the shop "feels" busy. Small groups of workers will suddenly stop talking to each other and will disperse, as if they were little schoolboys discovered sneaking a cigarette. Workers spend inordinate amounts of time "waiting" for work to arrive at their work-station. There are few, if any, pallets of work-in-process on the floor for each worker, and the workers are stretching out each job to avoid the inevitable layoff. These are the tell-tale signs of a shop not busy.

At one company where I was assessing the situation for an anxious owner, we were taking just such a walk through his shop when we passed a closed door. I asked him what was behind the door, and I was told it was just a materials storage room. I asked if I could look inside. When the door was opened, the light was on revealing a startled and embarrassed employee sitting on a stool with his feet up on a table, reading a newspaper. "I'm just between jobs," he mumbled, "the next job will be coming up soon." The work load had been insufficient to keep this man occupied, and he had found a novel hiding place.

The fourth method is simply to compare the direct labor dollars per dollar of sales for the past five years, and determine how badly the labor efficiency has slipped. Again, this parameter is sensitive to product and product mix changes. Of course, when you ask a typical supervisor how many people can be let go and still get the necessary work done, the supervisor will invariably point out that the company can't afford to lose anyone. The decision to lay off hourly employees is never straightforward, and is always unpopular. There are no scientific methods to determine how many workers to lay off. Good judgement and common sense must prevail.

Comparing the Past to the Present

The main objective of a turnaround is not necessarily to maximize the income of the company while minimizing its costs, but to optimize its profitability. What this really means is that it is better to end up with a company which only sells $20 million a year with a net profit of $1 million, than to have a company which sells $30 million a year and only nets $500 000. Although this may seem obvious, the concept is not universally practised.

The underlying assumption when analyzing a turnaround situation is that at one time the company was profitable. Management must have been doing something right in the past. If it is no longer profitable, then something must have changed. This "something" could be external forces or internal influences, and may be a combination of both.

An analysis, therefore, must include a study of what the company was like or what it was doing when it was successful, and comparing those parameters with the current situation. One should then be able to isolate the conditions which have changed, whether they are external or internal, and set about altering those conditions where practical or possible, to set a new course toward recovery.

The most practical place to begin an examination of the troubled company is with its financial position. There are two fundamental documents that are required for this examination: the Balance Sheet and the Statement of Earnings. Wherever possible, year-end statements should be audited statements. Year-to-date statements will be unaudited and therefore subject to question and some change. Consistent with the premise that the company was successful and profitable at one time in the past, it is necessary to compare all current and previous statements with at least one, and preferably several from the "good" years. The more detailed the comparison, the better the chances of being able to identify the factors causing the failure of the company.

In this chapter, we shall concern ourselves with the Statements of Earnings. An ideal comparison might be set up with the following headings:

Line Item	Audited Year End		Audited Year End Year 1		Audited Year End repeat for Years 2, 3 and 4		Unaudited Year-to-date Current Year	
	$	%	$	%	$	%	$	%
Net Sales		100		100		100		100

The most useful basis for comparison of the statements of earnings is to use "per cent of net sales" for each line item. "Net sales" represents gross sales less returns and discounts. When analyzing the statements of earnings, and when comparing previous years to each other and to the present in order to determine where the major changes have occurred, there are three factors to keep in mind:

1. Did the accounting method change during the ensuing period? If it did, the comparison may not yield valid results. Occasionally, the analysis reveals that certain accounts were lumped together in the past which are currently separated, or vice-versa. This can completely throw off a detailed comparison unless one has been forewarned.

2. Was the bookkeeper consistent in the application of the code of accounts? Inexplicable or unusual variances in particular accounts could simply be the result of mis-applying the code of accounts, and placing the expenditure into the wrong account. New personnel and temporary personnel can easily make this type of error, and things are not always what they seem.

3. Was the product line or the sales mix roughly constant during the period under examination? If not, the comparison will lose much of its meaning unless these variations are duly noted.

Assuming that the data can be manipulated in order to reasonably compare the line items from year to year, it should not take long to determine what, if anything, has changed. Which line items have gone out of control, and to what extent. A typical Statement of Earnings format is shown in Figure 1 (next page).

This analysis is the easy part. The more difficult task is to set up the detailed schedules of expenses. For smaller companies, past schedules are generally found in the auditor's report. For the current year, the accounting staff should be following the same format as was used in previous years, and the information should be readily available for all closed-out months. In small companies in financial difficulty, however, month-end closings are sometimes delayed for several weeks, and recent data is difficult to obtain. This may be due in part because there is insufficient personnel to perform all the necessary analyses in a short time, and also in part because sometimes the owners wish to manipulate the data to make the picture a little brighter.

One popular practice used by inventive business people to maintain their company's line of credit when the financial picture is sagging, is to close out the month-end costs slightly prior to the month-end sales. For example, if Company XYZ incurred its "normal" costs of $250 000 during the financial period 1 April through 30 April, but realized "unexpectedly slow" sales of only $220 000 during the same period, then obviously the resulting loss might affect the company's line of credit with its bank. By employing "creative accounting" the business person may decide to close out the month on 29 April for all incurred costs, and to keep the month open until 10 May for all sales. Reduced costs and increased sales will significantly improve the situation as far as the lending institution is concerned. This practice would not knowingly be accepted by a reputable auditor, and is indeed fraudulent. It is, however, quite common within smaller companies experiencing financial difficulties.

Figure 1: A Typical Statement of Earnings

| | Year One | | repeat for Years Two thru Five | |
	$	%	$	%
NET SALES		100.0		100.0
Beginning Inventory				
Raw Materials Purchases				
Ending Inventory				
Cost of Materials				
Direct Labor				
Manufacturing Overheads				
COST OF GOODS SOLD				
GROSS MARGIN				
Selling Expenses				
Administration Expenses				
Financial Expenses				
Development Expenses				
R & D Credits				
TOTAL EXPENSES				
Extraordinary Expenses				
EARNINGS BEFORE TAXES				
Income Taxes – current				
Income Taxes – deferred				
NET EARNINGS				
Retained Earnings, beginning				
Dividends				
Retained Earnings, end				

The practice will, of course, catch up to the players, because at some point during the year prior to the year-end audit, the cut-off points for costs and for sales must be brought back into line. The greater the gap, the greater the final shock. The astute turnaround person must quickly determine whether the month-end cut-off dates are real and consistent, if the cost comparisons month-to-month and against prior years are to be meaningful. Obviously, April's sales this year versus last year cannot be compared if the cut-off dates are not the same.

The standard detailed schedule of expenses may vary in the extent of its detail, but generally speaking all companies large and small should have similar expense headings. The real question is whether the bookkeepers and payables clerks in the smaller companies have the training, the ability and the patience to apply a detailed code of accounts to every incoming invoice, so that it can be meticulously assigned to the correct cost heading. Typical schedule of expenses formats are given in Figures 2 and 3 (following pages). A patient study of these detailed expenses, comparing past years to the current situation, can provide a wealth of information to the turnaround person. Those areas where the costs have risen disproportionately against sales will be immediately highlighted.

The ultimate problem for the turnaround person is to determine what the cost level for each line item should be. The fact that a particular line item cost has risen twice as fast as sales is not necessarily unusual or unexpected. It is quite conceivable that in order to increase sales, the company has had to incur sales representatives' training costs, increased personnel hiring fees, installation of additional phones, and higher long distance fax bills, and initially these costs could be quite disproportionate to the rise in sales. The company president or controller will always have excellent reasons why the costs are what they are, and every cost can be justified. But the fact is that the company is in financial trouble, and the costs will have to be cut. Period. The questions are only where, how and by how much?

Figure 2: A Detailed Schedule of Manufacturing Overheads and Selling Expenses.

	Month 1	complete for each month of the year	Total Year 1

MFG. OVERHEADS
Supervision
Clerical
Engineering
Indirect Labor
     – Maintenance
     – Quality Control
     – Cleaning
Fringe Benefits @ 25%
Contracts
     – Engineering
     – Maintenance
Sub-Contracted Mfg.
Worker's Compensation
Utilities
Maintenance parts
     – Factory
     – Equipment
Supplies & Small Tools
Shipping Materials
Transport
     – In
     – Out
Rent – Factory portion
Depreciation

SELLING EXPENSES
Salaries
Clerical
Fringe Benefits @ 25%
Commissions
Agents Fees
Professional Fees
Travel & Entertainment
Automobiles
Promotions
Advertising
Videos
Catalogs & Brochures
Trade Shows
Training Seminars
Royalty Payment
Depreciation

Figure 3: A Detailed Schedule of Administrative, Development and Financial Expenses

	Month 1	complete for each month of the year	Total Year 1
ADMIN. EXPENSES			
Management			
Clerical & Administration			
Fringe benefits @ 25%			
Incentives & Bonuses			
Management Fees			
Professional Fees			
Travel & Entertainment			
Automobiles			
Rent – Office Portion			
Telephone & Fax			
Postage & Printing			
Office Supplies			
Computer Supplies			
Office Equipment Leases			
Legal Fees			
Audit Fees			
Group Health Insurance			
Key Employee Insurance			
Business Insurance			
Business Taxes			
Dues & Subscriptions			
General Expense			
Bad Debts			
Depreciation			
DEVELOPMENT EXPENSES			
Management			
Engineering & Technical			
Labor			
Clerical			
Fringe benefits @ 25%			
Sub-contracts			
Professional Fees			
Materials			
Patent costs			
FINANCIAL EXPENSES			
Interest on Long Term Loans			
Interest on Short Term Loans			
Bank Charges			

The Turnaround Experience 43

Once the comparison of each line item is made between current cost levels and those of the past, it will become reasonably obvious where the expenses have gone out of control, if indeed they have. There will be no indication of WHY these costs are high; only that they ARE high. The person charged with the turnaround will now have two tasks to perform: to determine why certain areas have gone out of control, and then to decide what to do about it.

Determining what happened to permit costs to escalate disproportionately is a matter of talking to the various managers and department heads in the company, to discover what their intentions were, and to understand all the reasons why they acted as they did. What were their objectives, and who provided these objectives? Which costs were within their control, and which were the result of uncontrollable externally imposed increases?

It is quite possible that costs were indeed held within budgeted limits, and all department managers did their jobs well, but that the anticipated sales simply did not materialize. It can be argued that astute management should have anticipated this problem, and should have reduced the departmental budgets accordingly. But often the expenditures are made before it is realized that the sales will be slower than expected, and it is then too late to alter the budgets. Management should react as soon as it realises that costs are out of line with revenues, but this "after the fact" action often requires drastic measures involving cutting staff, dropping projects already underway and postponing important programs.

The difficult part for the turnaround person is to avoid becoming deeply involved in the explanations, to the point where he becomes committed to the status quo. It is deceptively easy to adopt the perspective of the existing management, and to find one's self agreeing that the current situation was unavoidable and there is little that can be done about it. The turnaround expert must remain dispassionate, skeptical and, most importantly, must be able to discern where management went wrong and where the decisions should have been made differently. He or she must refrain from becoming emotionally involved with the personnel, the company, the policies, the customers, the suppliers and the industry. He or she must be able to choose unpopular courses of action, smash sacred cows, disappoint committed managers, replace or let go management personnel, abolish management positions and set about to coldly rebuild the company from the top down.

A useful rule of thumb when attempting to restructure a company during a turnaround is that the ideal company should operate with only variable costs. There should be no fixed costs. The closer a company can come to realizing this goal, the greater the chances of survival during times of financial strain. Obviously, if the company can achieve the enviable position of possessing only variable costs, then an astute and fast-acting management can vary the cost structure downwards to counter-balance dropping income levels. It is therefore the general aim of any turnaround to restructure the company in such a way as to maximize the variability of its costs.

How does one go about converting fixed costs to variable costs? In some cases, it is clearly impossible. In others, it may be possible, but clearly impractical. A company which rents its premises under a long term lease will have no reasonable way of turning its rental obligations into a truly variable cost. The closest it can come would be to sub-let any available space if (a) there were any available space, (b) if the lease permitted sub-letting and (c) if there were a willing sub-lessee.

On the other hand, there are some areas where costs are traditionally considered fixed or semi-variable, which can be made considerably more variable. One of these is technical and managerial staff. Typically, companies hire full-time permanent employees to perform these functions. When times become tough, the salaries and fringe benefits of these line and staff personnel become burdens to the company, but they are kept on for traditional reasons. They are considered indispensable to the company. They are considered irreplaceable. It is feared that if key personnel is let go during a company "downsizing" it will be lost forever, to the ultimate detriment of the company.

But current thinking regarding technical and managerial staff is slowly changing. These people are more and more being looked upon as a commodity, to be contracted on and off as the corporate needs dictate. There exist today agencies which specialize in the contracting out of highly qualified personnel such as design engineers, technicians and managers, many of whom specialize in specific industries. These personnel are available on contract for short periods of a few months to long periods lasting several years. When they are no longer required by the hiring company, they are simply returned to the agency. The company pays no termination benefits, nor does it pay any unnecessary salaries.

This growing system of "renting talent" is not easy on the human population. The people in question have little or no stability in their lives. They are shunted from company to company, often in different regions of the country, for indeterminate periods of time. Job security and stable family lives are becoming elusive quantities as companies increasingly turn to contracting their management and technical needs. But the turnaround person has no time to consider the human cost of his or her actions. He or she is there for only one reason: to do what it takes to save the troubled company.

Of course, one can sometimes be wrong. I was working to turn around one company where the master mechanic was an absolute genius at maintaining the equipment in running order. When he saw what I was doing with the company, he decided to quit and look for greener pastures. No one else in the company could hold a candle to the master mechanic's ability to keep the plant operating efficiently. And I was never able to locate anyone from the outside to emulate his uncanny knack of keeping the machines running. He was truly one of a kind, and the plant lost a full 8 to 10 percentage points in operating efficiency simply due to his departure. I was never able to convince the master mechanic to return, and in the end, the plant did not recover from his loss. Not everyone is truly replaceable.

Another area which is difficult to control is the cost of long distance telephone calls. Many companies rely upon the integrity and honesty of their employees to keep the indiscriminate use of the long distance telephone to a minimum. Even honest employees, when confronted with the phone bill, can shake their heads incredulously and say, "I didn't think I talked that long!" Phone companies will, for very little cost, install systems which will limit the number of phones from which long distance calls can be made. They can require that the person placing the call give his personal code number to the operator before a long distance call can be connected. Each month, a report is sent to the company indicating each person who placed a call, the phone number called, how many minutes the call lasted and the cost of the call. Company management can then study these reports, determine whether the calls were justified, and take appropriate action when necessary. This simple procedure can cut thousands of dollars off the phone bills each month even in a medium sized company.

As part of the analysis of the company's cost structure, the turnaround person must ask over and over, what programs can be cut? Which managerial, technical and clerical positions can be cut, and still permit the efficient operation of the company? What surplus equipment can I sell for cash? Which cost items can be cut? How can they be reduced? How can the control mechanisms over the various cost items be improved?

The turnaround person's life revolves around thinking about ways to cut costs, to cut corners, to reduce staff and get the most "bang for the buck." It becomes a way of life. After a number of years of thinking in this manner, the typical turnaround person begins to lead a monastic corporate life, shunning company functions such as employee dinners, dances, golf tournaments and family picnics as no more than a waste of corporate funds.

It is for this reason that many turnaround persons have difficulty in situations where the launching of a new product line requires the expenditure of considerable sums of speculative and promotional funds. Marketing costs are viewed with suspicion, and eventually all expenditures are examined with a Scrooge-like eye. The turnaround person must ensure that he or she does not fall into the trap of cutting all costs to the bone, and not allowing the company to breathe.

I lived through one turnaround situation where the company's financial management was in such a zealous mood to cut all expenditures, that they did not ask the phone company to provide a bridging service when the company changed its address. For several weeks, customers were unable to call the order desk, and some of them became convinced the company had gone out of business!

If a company is to survive, to rebuild its place in the market, and to grow beyond what it was before, then certain funds will have to be allocated to promote this growth. The turnaround person will have to exhibit considerable judgement in order to provide the balance necessary to cut with one hand and provide with the other.

Financial and Other Indicators of Health

The next step after studying the company's costs and comparing them with the past, is to take the "pulse" of the company with whatever tools are available. The most common and most useful tools are the balance sheet, various financial ratios and productivity indexes.

The balance sheet is probably the most difficult part of the puzzle to analyze. The fundamental question is whether the information can be taken at face value, or whether a certain amount of interpretation must be undertaken. Certain aspects of the balance sheet will be straightforward, such as the bank indebtedness; the line of credit used can be verified by the bank. But other areas will be open to question, and must be approached with caution. A typical balance sheet is shown in Figure 4 (following page).

Some of the areas that require caution when performing an analysis of the balance sheet are the following:

(a) Accounts Receivable

The turnaround person must take the trouble to determine whether all the accounts noted under this heading are indeed collectible. Some of the accounts may in fact belong to defunct or bankrupt companies, and will never be collected. Others may belong to companies which are in financial difficulty, and may be over 120 days old and more rightly called "doubtful accounts." Banks do not acknowledge receivables over 90 days, and will not permit aged receivables over 90 days in the calculation of a line of credit.

Figure 4: A Typical Small to Mid-Size Company Balance Sheet

	Year 1	Year 2	Year 3	Year 4	Year 5

ASSETS

CURRENT ASSETS
Cash
Accounts Receivable
Inventories
Income Tax Credits
R & D Tax Credits
Grants Receivable
Pre-paid Expenses

Net Fixed Assets
Advances to
    Shareholders
Deferred Development
    Costs
Patents
Goodwill

LIABILITIES

CURRENT LIABILITIES
Bank Indebtedness
Accounts Payable
Current Portion, Long
    Term Debt
Current Portion, Long
    Term Leases
Income Taxes Payable

LONG TERM DEBT
Bank Loan
Long Term Lease
    Obligations
Shareholders' Loan

**SHAREHOLDERS'
EQUITY**
Share Capital
Retained Earnings

Some accounts may be under dispute. An argument arising out of questionable quality, the wrong price, late shipment or other problem may be holding up payment, and if the dispute is sufficiently serious the payment may never be made unless court action is taken.

It would not be unusual to discover that less than 80% of the stated accounts receivable are truly receivable. The receivables clerks generally know the exact status of each account, and can be counted upon as reliable sources of information. The turnaround expert is faced with the dilemma: whether to write off the uncollectible receivables, which will result in a worse balance sheet; or to maintain the inflated receivables and know they will never be collected. The company's auditors will resolve this dilemma in any case.

(b) Inventories

As has already been noted, the inventories heading can be a real "dog's breakfast." This heading generally contains all three inventory types, namely raw materials, work-in-process and finished goods.

It must be determined whether all the raw materials are current, and are of the quality and grade required for foreseeable production schedules. Discontinued products can leave a company with whole silos or storage bins full of raw materials which will never be usable. Often companies possess entire categories of raw materials such as hardware items or various mechanical or electrical components which are slow movers, which have been in inventory for years, and which show little or no inclination to move in the foreseeable future. Often these items are on the books at full or close to full value.

The work-in-process inventories may be quarantined due to machining errors, or set aside due to changes in a customer's requirements, and possibly should be considered closer to scrap than to an active inventory. Some finished goods may be damaged due to poor handling and storage habits, or may be obsolete, off-quality or simply an overrun which was held for a customer but never shipped. While some of this inventory may be saleable at close to full value, other parts of it may not sell even to a jobber or a scrap dealer.

It is the unenviable task of the turnaround expert to quickly evaluate the status of the company's inventories. Usually, a supervisor who does not particularly like the existing management will be the best source of information on all the flaws in the company's inventories. Storeskeepers, too, know their inventories by heart, and can tell quickly which items move and which do not.

The dilemma for the turnaround person is the following: if the inventories are devalued, the asset base diminishes. If the inventories are devalued and then some sold off, a profit will be shown for the transaction. If the inventories are not devalued and some sold off at less than book value, much needed cash can be obtained, but a loss will be shown for the transaction.

If the inventory levels drop too low, then the line of credit will suffer, since the banks generally recognize up to 50% of the saleable work-in-process inventories and 75% of finished goods inventories as the basis for the company's line of credit. Thus it may prove expedient to maintain inventories at a high level. In any case, the ultimate valuation of the inventories must withstand the scrutiny of auditors.

(c) Net Fixed Assets

This category is difficult to assess, because the valuation of an asset for "book" purposes depends upon the rate of depreciation which was allowed by the government or by the auditors. The book value may bear no significant relationship to the market value. And in some cases, "market value" may be close to the scrap value. In certain cases where the fixed assets are truly undervalued, it is possible to have the auditing firm re-value the assets.

(d) Accounts Payable

It is important to separate the trade payables from other payables. In smaller companies for example, a shareholder may have a loan outstanding which is shown as a payable. During times of financial difficulty it is extremely unlikely that such a loan would be repaid, and it should be clearly separated from those payables which will be honored inside the next six months.

Once the turnaround person has carefully reviewed the balance sheets, and is satisfied that the information contained therein is correct, valid and representative of the facts, and that he or she truly understands what is contained in each of the headings, then and only then can the evaluation of the real health of the company begin.

In one small company where I was asked to manage a turnaround, the owner had recently hired his wife as the chief accountant. Her original training had been in the social sciences. She was an intelligent woman, quick to learn in difficult situations, and had absorbed much of the task of the chief accountant in a very short time. When I first joined the company, I asked for an up-to-date balance sheet so I could better assess the company's financial position. The very next day I received on my desk a page totalling assets and liabilities. It took only a quick glance to realize that the totals were not equal, and it was jokingly known ever after as the "unbalance sheet." Getting balance sheets to balance is not always an easy task, and very often the accountant in charge will resort to "plugging" certain numbers in order to make the figures balance. Inventory figures are often modified slightly, to turn unbalance sheets into balance sheets.

The following are some of the more important and key ratios for the turnaround person to calculate and to track, in order to evaluate the health of the company. These ratios and percentages should be continuously monitored, in order to evaluate whether progress is being made toward a recovery, or whether the recovery efforts are ineffective.

i. The Current Ratio

The current ratio represents the surplus of short term liquidity over short term debts. The ratio is used as an indication of the availability of a company's working capital, and represents the company's ability to pay its wages, its trade payables and its financial obligations. The ratio is expressed as current assets divided by current liabilities, and historically a ratio of 2:1 or higher is considered ideal. The company in financial difficulty rarely has a current ratio in excess of 1:1, and 0.5:1 is certainly not uncommon. Average current ratios for various industries in the early 1990s are shown in Figure 5 (following page).

Figure 5: Average Current Ratios by Industry

For Medium-sized companies with assets between $1 and $5 million.
Source: Financial Survey of Canadian Business Performance, CCH Canadian Limited, 1990.

Aircraft Parts Manufacturers	1.39
Bakeries	0.94
Distilleries	1.69
Clothing Manufacturers	1.98
Commercial Printers	1.14
Industrial Electrical Equipment Manufacturers	1.69
Food Industries	1.31
Glass Products Manufacturers	1.64
Home Furniture Manufacturers	1.55
Radio & TV Manufacturers	1.30
Industrial Chemicals Manufacturers	0.90
Machine Shops	2.28
Major Appliance Manufacturers	1.51
Metal Stamping	1.38
Automotive Accessories Manufacturers	1.60
Pharmaceuticals Manufacturers	1.63
Plastic Parts Manufacturers	1.15
Rubber Manufacturers	1.30
Shoe Manufacturers	1.07
Textile Manufacturers	1.83

ii. The Quick Ratio

The quick ratio is similar to the current ratio, except that inventories have been excluded from the current assets. This is done because inventories are not always a guaranteed source of quick cash. In fact, in a troubled company a considerable portion of the inventories are likely to be obsolete, off-standard or generally un-saleable. Therefore, the quick ratio may be more representative of the financially troubled company's ability to generate working capital than is the traditional current ratio.

iii. Accounts Receivable Days

If one takes the estimated annual credit sales (i.e. all sales other than cash sales) and divides that number by 360, one then has an approximation of the average sales per day. Taking the accounts receivable and dividing by the average sales per day, one obtains the equivalent number of days of receivables the company has outstanding. In good times, this number can be 30 days. As it becomes harder to collect one's receivables this number can climb to 60 days, and in extreme cases can exceed 90 days. The higher the number, the greater the indication that the company is having trouble collecting its receivables, and the greater the emphasis which must be placed on the credit and collections functions.

iv. Accounts Payable Days

In the same way as the accounts receivable days are calculated, the outstanding accounts payable figure is divided by the average purchases per day (raw materials, sub-contracts and supplies), to yield an accounts payable days outstanding number. If the accounts payable days are lower than the accounts receivable days, this means that the company is paying its suppliers faster than its customers are paying their debts. This is a sure way to quickly drain the company's cash resources. Ideally, the payables days should equal or even exceed the receivables days, and the extent to which this can be done represents the ability of management to manage the firm's cash during hard times.

iv. Gross Margin

The gross margin is what is left over after the cost of goods sold is removed from net sales, which are generally calculated as gross sales less discounts and returns. The gross margin by itself is meaningless, and can vary with the industry. Typical gross margins range from 20% to 40% or even higher. Simply stated, the gross margin must permit sufficient gross profit to pay for administrative costs, selling costs, financial expenses, development costs and allow something left over for a reasonable profit. The turnaround specialist must determine what a normal gross margin should be for the particular industry, and then monitor the company's gross margin continuously to determine that it is heading in the right direction. Average gross margins for various industries are shown in Figure 6 (following page).

Figure 6: Average Gross Margin Percent By Industry

For Medium-sized companies with assets between $1 and $5 million.
Source: Financial Survey of Canadian Business Performance, CCH Canadian Limited, 1990.

Aircraft Parts Manufacturers	26.2%
Bakeries	27.7
Distilleries	20.2
Clothing Manufacturers	22.5
Commercial Printers	37.6
Industrial Electrical Equipment Manufacturers	25.8
Food Industries	20.7
Glass Products Manufacturers	24.6
Home Furniture Manufacturers	25.8
Radio & TV Manufacturers	22.7
Industrial Chemicals Manufacturers	24.5
Machine Shops	45.9
Major Appliance Manufacturers	26.4
Metal Stamping	28.0
Automotive Accessories Manufacturers	23.1
Pharmaceuticals Manufacturers	30.2
Plastic Parts Manufacturers	27.3
Rubber Manufacturers	18.9
Shoe Manufacturers	25.2
Textile Manufacturers	26.2

v. Inventory Turns

Inventory should always be valued at the cost of goods sold, which includes only materials, utilities, direct labor and manufacturing overheads. If one takes the estimated annual cost of goods sold and divides this figure by the current inventories, the resulting number represents the number of times the inventories turn over in a year.

$$\frac{\text{Annual Cost-of-goods-sold}}{\text{Inventory value}} = \text{Inventory Turns}$$

The absolute number by itself means very little. Inventory turns will depend upon the type of industry, and normal inventory turns can run from 4 times per year in heavy industrial settings to as high as 20 for perishable foodstuffs. Average inventory turns by industry are shown in Figure 7. It is necessary for the turnaround person to be familiar with the typical turns for a particular industry. It is important to understand that the inventories represent sunk costs which are lying dormant. The higher the turns the better, and the lower the inventories the better.

Figure 7: Average Inventory Turns by Industry

For Medium-sized companies with assets between $1 and $5 million.
Source: Financial Survey of Canadian Business Performance, CCH Canadian Limited, 1990.

Aircraft Parts Manufacturers	5.0
Bakeries	15.4
Distilleries	3.7
Clothing Manufacturers	2.2
Commercial Printers	8.4
Industrial Electrical Equipment Manufacturers	3.6
Food Industries	5.6
Glass Products Manufacturers	4.6
Home Furniture Manufacturers	4.2
Radio & TV Manufacturers	3.7
Industrial Chemicals Manufacturers	8.2
Machine Shops	10.7
Major Appliance Manufacturers	3.8
Metal Stamping	7.8
Automotive Accessories Manufacturers	5.8
Pharmaceuticals Manufacturers	3.4
Plastic Parts Manufacturers	4.9
Rubber Manufacturers	4.3
Shoe Manufacturers	3.9
Textile Manufacturers	3.5

Ideally, inventory turns should be calculated separately for each of the three basic inventory categories, and each ratio monitored on its own. Historical information, going back to the years when the company was profitable, should act as a guide when targeting where the inventory turnover ratios should lie. Unfortunately, inventory turns by themselves do not necessarily tell the whole story. Often only a small portion of the inventory turns over rapidly, while a significant portion may not move at all. While the global inventory turnover figure may appear encouraging, the turnaround person must always be vigilant for dead or obsolete stock.

vi. Expense Ratios

It is mandatory that the turnaround person take each of the major expense headings in the Statement of Earnings reports, and represent them as a percent of Net Sales. At the very least, these headings would be the following:

* Raw Materials
* Direct Labor
* Manufacturing Overheads
* Administrative Expenses
* Selling Expenses
* Financial Expenses
* R & D Expenses

Each of these elements can be further subdivided if some of the key expenses are worth tracking. For example, the cost of managers' salaries, telephone expenses, the cost of energy and utilities, or any single item which bears monitoring.

vii. Debt to Equity Ratios

Fortunate indeed is the company which has rarely or never relied on long term investment to supply the cash for operations. Heavy equipment purchases, expansion into new product lines, or even opening up branch plants demands a heavy investment which can rarely be paid out of earnings. The amount of long term debt will usually determine the extent of future borrowing power. There are two ways which are often used to decide the borrowing power of a company:

(a) Total Debt to Equity

The Total Debt is simply the Current Liabilities plus the Long Term Liabilities. When this Total Debt is divided by the Shareholders' Equity (Total Assets less Total Liabilities), the resulting ratio is an indicator of the borrowing strength of the company. A ratio as high as 3:1 usually means trouble, and a lending institution will not seriously consider a long term loan. Even a ratio of 2:1 will be examined carefully before any action is contemplated toward making a loan.

(b) Long Term Debt to Equity

This ratio is the Long Term Liabilities divided by the Shareholders' Equity. A ratio of 1:1 is considered reasonably healthy, and higher ratios will require close examination before a lending institution will consider a long term loan. In each of these cases, the exact ratios will depend upon the industry sector, and must be considered in the proper context. Typical values for various industries are shown in Figure 8.

Figure 8: Average Long Term Debt To Equity Ratios by Industry

For Medium-sized companies with assets between $1 and $5 million.
Source: Financial Survey of Canadian Business Performance, CCH Canadian Limited, 1990.

Aircraft Parts Manufacturers	0.6:1
Bakeries	0.9:1
Distilleries	0.4:1
Clothing Manufacturers	0.5:1
Commercial Printers	0.6:
Industrial Electrical Equipment Manufacturers	0.6:1
Food Industries	0.6:1
Glass Products Manufacturers	0.6:1
Home Furniture Manufacturers	0.9:1
Radio & TV Manufacturers	0.4:1
Industrial Chemicals Manufacturers	0.4:1
Machine Shops	1.1:1
Major Appliance Manufacturers	0.3:1
Metal Stamping	0.6:1
Automotive Accessories Manufacturers	0.6:1
Pharmaceuticals Manufacturers	1.4:1
Plastic Parts Manufacturers	0.8:1
Rubber Manufacturers	0.3:1
Shoe Manufacturers	0.2:1
Textile Manufacturers	0.6:1

viii. Interest Coverage Ratio (EBIT/I)

One often-used measure of the market value of a company, either currently or on a pro-forma basis, is a simple EBIT multiple. The EBIT is calculated as the Earnings Before Interest charges and income Taxes. The multiple depends upon the industry, but normally ranges between 4 and 8. This is a "quick and dirty" method of evaluating the market value of a company when calculating a potential investor's return after a set number of years.

The EBIT can also be divided by the company's interest charges to yield the interest coverage ratio. A normal value for this ratio might be 2 or higher. In most cases, a financially troubled company will have little or no positive earnings, and the interest coverage ratio could drop to .25 or lower, indicating trouble. Some interest coverage ratios for various industries are shown in Figure 9.

Figure 9: Average Interest Coverage Ratios by Industry

For Medium-sized companies with assets between $1 and $5 million.
Source: Financial Survey of Canadian Business Performance, CCH Canadian Limited, 1990.

	EBIT as % of sales	INT as % of sales	EBIT/I
Aircraft Parts Manufacturers	10.8	2.9	3.7
Bakeries	5.8	1.6	3.6
Distilleries	12.6	0.4	31.5
Clothing Manufacturers	6.1	1.8	3.4
Commercial Printers	6.6	1.0	6.6
Industrial Electrical Equipment Mfrs.	4.8	1.3	3.7
Food Industries	5.7	0.6	9.5
Glass Products Manufacturers	7.1	1.4	5.1
Home Furniture Manufacturers	4.5	1.9	2.4
Radio & TV Manufacturers	4.1	0.8	5.1
Industrial Chemicals Manufacturers	14.7	0.2 7	3.5
Machine Shops	8.3	3.2	2.6
Major Appliance Manufacturers	11.5	1.4	8.2
Metal Stamping	7.5	0.7	10.7
Automotive Accessories Manufacturers	7.0	1.2	5.8
Pharmaceuticals Manufacturers	7.7	1.9	4.1
Plastic Parts Manufacturers	7.4	1.8	4.1
Rubber Manufacturers	6.5	0.9	7.2
Shoe Manufacturers	3.2	1.8	1.8
Textile Manufacturers	5.5	1.5	3.7

ix. Return on Assets

The return on assets is calculated as the Net Profits after Taxes divided by the Total Assets, and expressed as a percentage. The figure by itself is not particularly meaningful, except inasmuch as it tells the company owners whether they might not have been better off investing in blue-chip stocks or high quality bonds.

x. Return on Sales

The return on sales is calculated as the Net Profits after Taxes divided by the Net Sales, and expressed as a percentage. Both the Return on Assets and the Return on Sales become more meaningful when compared to the industry average. Average net incomes after taxes are shown as a percent of sales for various industries in Figure 10.

Figure 10: Average Net Income After Taxes As A Percent Of Sales by Industry

For Medium-sized companies with assets between $1 and $5 million.
Source: Financial Survey of Canadian Business Performance, CCH Canadian Limited, 1990.

Aircraft Parts Manufacturers	5.0
Bakeries	2.0
Distilleries	9.0
Clothing Manufacturers	3.0
Commercial Printers	4.0
Industrial Electrical Equipment Manufacturers	2.0
Food Industries	3.0
Glass Products Manufacturers	3.0
Home Furniture Manufacturers	1.0
Radio & TV Manufacturers	2.0
Industrial Chemicals Manufacturers	15.0
Machine Shops	3.0
Major Appliance Manufacturers	5.0
Metal Stamping	5.0
Automotive Accessories Manufacturers	3.0
Pharmaceuticals Manufacturers	2.0
Plastic Parts Manufacturers	3.0
Rubber Manufacturers	2.0
Shoe Manufacturers	1.0
Textile Manufacturers	3.0

6

Judging the Human Side of the Business

People tend to anthropomorphise companies. We speak of a company being generous, a company that that pays attention to quality or a company that listens to its employees, and so on. In truth, of course, a company is nothing more than a legal entity and is made up of people. These people who make up a company are simply a group of separate individuals, each with a set of needs and problems, acting with some relatively common purpose under the umbrella of a legal name.

The personality which we ascribe to a given company is generally a reflection of the top executive. The nature, personality, attention to detail and degree of concern for the quality of the product and the needs of the employees, will normally be radiated downward from this person through the organization. This is particularly true in a small to medium sized company, where most of the personnel will be exposed to some extent to the senior person on a fairly regular basis. His or her personality will "rub off" on the employees. In a large corporation this is less obvious, and the personality of the company becomes a reflection of the group of senior executives. But even here, the top executives have a great deal to say in the choice of their immediate subordinates, and so their influence, although indirect, is still very real.

We expect this senior executive, or group of senior executives, to steer the company on a steady upward course of growth and profitability, no matter what the storms that may rage around them. We expect them to hire the right people. We expect them to effectively face down the competition, to manage through the recessions, to launch innovative products at the right time and to ensure an efficient operation.

In fact, we expect a lot from senior management, some of whom have received no formal education in management, and some of whom have only limited experience managing businesses through difficult times. It is precisely this senior management with whom the turnaround person first comes into contact. It is with this person or this group that the turnaround expert's first impression of the company and its problems is made.

The vast majority of troubled companies are in their predicament due to poor management. The senior executives did not foresee the problems, or did not react in time to avoid or to solve them. In the first meeting with the company board members, owners or senior executives, the turnaround specialist must attempt to size up their understanding of the problem: does anyone in the company understand (a) what happened, (b) why the problems exist and (c) what is to be done about it?

Generally, the senior management is in a state of shock. By the time the decision has been made to call in a turnaround expert, it may well be too late to save the company. At least, not without pouring more money into the sinking ship than the owners or creditors are willing to part with. This means that the task of defining the problem and determining its solution will fall squarely on the shoulders of the turnaround person.

In the smaller company the top executive is often the owner, and it has been my experience that the owner often says to the turnaround person, "I'm leaving on a holiday. I'll keep in touch with you. Let me know when you've turned it around," or words to that effect. In a larger organization, the president or equivalent will stay on, and will demand only periodic up-dates on the findings and the recommendations of the turnaround person.

In either case, the turnaround person must be left alone to carry out the investigations and to perform whatever tasks must be accomplished to effect the turnaround. This must be made perfectly clear to the hiring body. It has been my experience that the most effective method to operate is to be hired by the company as a direct employee, and to be given a high and fancy title, in order to have the necessary authority and power to effect whatever changes are necessary.

The task of assessing whether the senior managers of the company understand their functions, understand the nature of the problem and what caused it, and have a good grasp of the remedial action required, is the first order on the menu of the turnaround person. Evaluating the responses and the abilities of these senior people is, unfortunately, almost purely subjective. The turnaround expert must try to avoid being negative toward a manager just because there might exist a personality clash, or because the person in question cheers for the wrong baseball team.

The evaluation of the management team must be made quickly, and must be based upon the responses to the questions asked by the turnaround specialist. Questions about attitude towards the company and its senior executive; questions about solutions to the current problem; about willingness to work long hours, and to accept new ideas and radical solutions; questions which reveal general intelligence and degree of knowledge of the industry. Above all, questions which reveal the degree of resistance to change. And then, in arbitrary fashion, the turnaround person must decide whether the incumbent is suitable to continue in his or her job.

A turnaround is not a school for executives. There is no time to take the senior people by the hand and teach them how to perform their jobs better. The turnaround person must make a rapid judgement about whether the incumbent is capable of fitting into the new order, or whether that employee must be replaced. Period. The turnaround person may know of a capable replacement, but in general must deal through a trusted executive placement agency, and hire a replacement. Of course, the interviewing of prospective candidates must be done by the turnaround person, so that the desired characteristics and "fit" of the new executive is the best available.

Very often the turnaround person will have difficulty attracting an ideal candidate into the company. Word of the company's financial problems may already have spread through the business community, and it takes a certain adventuresome spirit to join a troubled company. In one assignment that I had, I had to interview 31 candidates for a general management position before I found an acceptable candidate who agreed to join the company. But this is highly unusual. Between half-a-dozen and a dozen is more usual.

In a small company, if the least competent executive of the group is the president or owner, then the turnaround person is caught in a dilemma. It may be possible to convince the president to step up to occupy the chairman's position, in order to allow an aggressive and qualified underling to take over as president. Another way to set an incompetent president aside is to suggest bringing into the company an equity partner with a sizable cash infusion, and who would be capable of acting as the new president. Whatever the attempted solution, the situation is extremely delicate, and there is no guarantee that the incompetent president will step aside. After due consideration, the turnaround person might decide to give up the mandate.

Another potential road-block sometimes faced by the turnaround person in a smaller company is the fact that one of the managers deemed incompetent might be a relative of the president or owner, or perhaps is a favorite employee who helped found the business and to whom the president wishes to remain loyal. I had been hired by a very successful company owner to make a subsidiary company profitable. The subsidiary had existed for many years under a general manager who helped found the subsidiary, but it had never, in all the years it had existed, turned a profit.

In my judgement, the major obstacle to profitability was the general manager. He seemed to have little understanding of product costing, and I judged his choice of accountants to be atrocious. I so informed the owner, and went about the matter of preparing to let the general manager go. To my utmost surprise, the owner burst into my office one morning and announced to me that there was no way that he was going to let go an old loyal employee, and that I was moving too quickly and that I was "ruffling too many feathers." And then he thanked me for my services and terminated my contract. That was the first and only time that I lost my job because I was proceeding too quickly with the turnaround!

Letting Go the Senior Manager

Dealing with the senior manager who is being let go is another matter. The humane thing to do would be to make every attempt to re-train the manager in question, so that he or she would eventually perform the job and fit into the new vision of the organization. Unfortunately, there is not generally the time to spend on training existing employees. A turnaround is essentially a race between the turnaround person and the bank manager, to determine whether the former can generate a profit before the latter decides to "pull the plug."

The turnaround person, whose distasteful task it is to inform the unfortunate executive of the decision, must patiently but firmly tell the fired executive to clear out personal effects, and leave the premises. The reactions of executives being dismissed vary from stoic acceptance and comments such as, "well, I knew it was coming," to stunned silence and even weeping. It is best for all concerned if the amount of time spent in saying good-byes is kept to an absolute minimum. All accrued salary, earned bonuses, expenses and vacation pay must be prepared in advance. In addition, a separation package must also be prepared. The amount of the separation package usually varies with the seniority of the position, the length of time the person worked for the company and the reason for the decision to let the person go. Unless the reasons for dismissal are sufficiently serious, such as provable fraud, the separation packages are made sufficiently large to avoid law suits for "wrongful dismissal." The amount can vary depending upon the province or state, and it is best for the turnaround person to consult with a reputable local legal firm before making any final decisions in this regard.

The executive must be required to sign a statement of discharge, indicating that the company owes no further remuneration, and that he or she gives up the right for any future legal action against the company. If the executive agrees to sign the discharge form, all the moneys owed are immediately handed over, and all good-byes are quickly said. If the executive opts not to sign the discharge form, only the final paycheque and all accrued expenses and vacation pay are given, and the separation pay is withheld. Obviously, there is going to be a court battle. A typical statement of discharge format is shown in Figure 11.

Figure 11: A Typical Executive Discharge Form
RECEIPT, RELEASE AND DISCHARGE

I, _____, by these presents hereby acknowledge to have received from my employer, _____, the sum of $_____ in full and final payment and settlement of any and all claims which I had, may have, or may pretend to have against my employer of any kind or nature whatsoever. In consideration of said payment I hereby forever release and discharge my employer, its assigns, agents and employees, and the heirs and representatives, with respect to any and all claims of any kind or nature which may have existed with respect to any relationship between the undersigned and my employer.

I further acknowledge that my employ with my employer is hereby terminated and I waive and renounce any and all claims relating thereto.

In consideration of the above-mentioned payment made to me, I grant unto my employer complete receipt, release and discharge and I waive any and all rights, real or otherwise, which I had, may have or may pretend to have against my employer in virtue of any and all relationships between ourselves, dealings or otherwise, and I hereby acknowledge that my employer owes no moneys of any kind or nature to me and that I have no claim whatsoever against my employer.

City:_____ Province:_____

Dated:_____ Signed:_____

One case I had to deal with involved an excellent, hard-working manager who had a serious drinking problem. His alcohol problem was interfering with his performance on the job, and I decided that he just had to go. I felt very badly about the decision, because the company was unable to afford the time and the money to rehabilitate the individual. In a sense, we were throwing him to the wolves.

But the company's cash situation was desperate, and we were facing a strike, and there was no room for sympathy.

The afternoon following his dismissal I received a call from the man's wife, who informed me that her husband had left their house with a pistol in his pocket. I had no idea what he intended to do with the pistol, but I could only assume that he was going to visit me at the office, and "settle accounts." So, I told all the office employees to go home, and I sat in my office and spent several anxious hours waiting for him. I waited until well past the office closing hours, but he never showed up. To this day, I have no idea what he intended to do with the pistol, but I was extremely relieved that it was not intended for me.

Happily, the great majority of dismissals are not so nerve-wracking.

A Close Look at the Organization

The next step for turnaround person is to study the existing corporate organization. It must be determined, first of all, whether the organization is hierarchical or horizontal, functional, nepotistic and whether it is suited to the organization at hand. Smaller companies very often do not even have formal organization charts, a fact that that makes the task of the turnaround person that much more difficult, because one must then be constructed from scratch.

Senior executives utilize many styles of management. I once had to deal with a president who said, "We don't have titles here. Everyone does whatever has to be done. We're all at the same level." However interesting and egalitarian this management principle may sound in theory, I have absolutely no doubt that when the boss demanded action, the organizational structure quickly assumed a hierarchical nature.

This lack of visible organizational structure can permeate all the way down to the supervisory level. In one turnaround situation that I was managing in a large company, I did interviews of employees at all levels in order to assess the magnitude of the problem. I spotted a worker who appeared to be wandering about somewhat aimlessly, and asked him, "Who do you work for?"

"Oh," he replied casually, "sometimes I work for Bill, and sometimes for George, and quite often for Frank."

"How can you work for three people at the same time?" I asked, dumbfounded. "Who tells you what to do?"

The worker looked at me with total disdain. "Son," he said, "I've been doing this job for over forty years. No one has to tell me what to do. I know what to do."

In the same company, when I asked a foreman how many workers he had on the job that day, he replied that he didn't know. I then asked him how many he was supposed to have working for him, to which he replied that he wasn't sure.

In yet another turnaround situation which I was piloting, the situation was even worse. Management had abdicated its right to manage years before, and the union had filled the vacuum left by management. The union decided how much production was going to be made each day, and the union decided how many employees were required to produce it. The foremen were told to stay in their offices, out of the way of the workers, and any foreman stupid enough to challenge the union would find himself surrounded by a rather ugly gang of toughs in the parking lot after work. The entire organization chart was nothing but a joke.

The task of the turnaround expert is to quickly decide what the "ideal" organization chart would look like for the company at hand. In essence, the ideal chart would have the least possible number of positions, with the least number of levels, and each box would be filled by the best possible candidate available to the turnaround person, whether from within the company or from without. The turnaround person must develop this ideal chart on paper, and then decide who should fill the boxes. Some of the boxes may be identical to those already in existence; but some would represent totally new jobs which bear little resemblance to current conditions.

For example, the existing organization may have a person in charge of New Product Development. The turnaround person may decide, however, that the company is too small to afford the luxury of a separate manager for this position, and that the function of New Product Development should be combined with another function, such as the Director of Marketing, at least until the company gets back on its feet. By the same token, however, the turnaround person must ensure that the person who fills the position of Director of Marketing is capable of handling new product development.

Another dilemma concerns nepotism. I have been involved in a turnaround of a division of a large company wherein many of the senior positions were occupied by relatives and friends of the owner. I knew some of these people, and although many of them were very nice individuals, I felt that they were not qualified for the positions which they held. It is very difficult to diplomatically tell a president/owner that the vice-president of procurement is not doing a good job, and is costing the company millions. Nonetheless, the turnaround person must be prepared to take the bull by the horns and pave the way for the needed changes, or the battle will be lost. Better to lose the contract, than to fail by trying to appease the owners or the top executive.

One aspect often forgotten when setting up a new and presumably tighter organization is to ensure that all incumbents, whether newly hired or old employees in new positions, understand clearly what the turnaround person has in mind. Nothing is more frustrating for the turnaround person than to place a person into a position, and two months later realize that the incumbent has not understood his or her new role, simply because the job was not adequately described to the incumbent in sufficient detail. People cannot do their jobs if they don't understand what is expected of them. This may sound obvious, but it is worth repeating.

In short, the turnaround person must ensure that the new organization is extremely lean; that every incumbent has a clearly written description of job responsibilities; that the incumbent has read and truly understands these responsibilities; and that each incumbent knows exactly how the position fits into the organization, and to whom reports should be made.

Writing detailed job descriptions is tedious work, but it is extremely important that everyone in the company know exactly what their job is. Some job descriptions are simply accounts of what the employee believes the job to be. But a real and proper job description should describe what the company requires of the individual, and if carefully prepared, can also be used to assess the relative pay scale of the position. Some typical job descriptions for various company positions are provided in APPENDIX II.

It is also an axiom of good management that all decisions should be made at the lowest possible level in the organization. It really is a waste of time for senior managers to worry about minor decisions, particularly if the impact of those decisions is only a few thousand dollars.

In one large multi-plant company for which I was managing a turnaround, there was a plant manager who simply would not grasp this simple principle. I remember vividly the occasion when he had to leave his plant for a few days to attend a meeting at Head Office. While he was absent, the plant suffered a prolonged power outage, and the process furnaces went cold. The plant engineer took matters into his hands, and did the best he could with a bad situation. When the plant manager returned after a few days, he noticed all the product which had been scrapped due to the power failure. The irate plant manager called the plant engineer into his office, and shouted at him, "In the future, when you've got a serious problem at the plant, don't try to think! Call me!"

The Nasty Side of Employees: Theft and Fraud

Almost everyone has heard horror stories of employees or their relatives driving up to the company loading dock at midnight and filling up their truck with valuable materials and products. I witnessed such a theft in broad daylight. A truck suddenly pulled up to our receiving dock. The driver jumped out, picked up a heavy aluminum casting, dumped it in the back of his truck, and took off at full speed. I was so shocked, I didn't think to call the police! In another instance, the offending employees had carried a large valuable motor to a remote section of the property fence, and were in the process of cutting a hole in the fence when they were discovered. In yet another company, I watched a stranger jump into an employee's truck, start it up, and drive away!

Another common method of theft is for employees to place small but expensive tools such as micrometers and vernier calipers in their lunch boxes, and take them home. The same trick is used to steal office supplies, and here the vehicle is the attache case. This is politely known by companies as "shrinkage."

Theft is a fact of life, and the turnaround person must ensure that sufficient measures are taken if theft is suspected. Lunch boxes and attache cases can be inspected, even though the action may be considered distasteful and degrading to the employees. Private investigators can be hired; "moles" can be hired into the workforce to spy on thieves, and closed circuit TV cameras can be trained on strategic exits and loading docks. Loathsome though it may be to take such drastic action, if employee theft has been proven to be contributing to company costs, it must be stopped.

Another common form of theft is the taking of valuables from offices, such as theft from the petty cash drawer, or cash from employees' purses which are left unattended. In one company where I was conducting a turnaround, we had our petty cash drawer broken into seven times. We had a good idea who was behind the break-ins, but we were never there to catch the thief. One of the detectives on the case suggested we use "blue dye." This dye comes in the form of a blue powder which, when in contact with moisture such as on a person's hands, melts and colors the hands indelibly. It takes days to wear off, and it cannot be washed off, even with the strongest lye soap.

We carefully sprinkled the blue dye powder on some bills, and carefully placed them in the petty cash box. Our suspect took the bait. The morning after the petty cash was stolen for the seventh and last time, he didn't show up for work. When I sent the detectives to his home to investigate the reason for his absence, they caught him red-handed. Or should I say, blue-handed.

Another more insidious form of theft is employees' use of drugs on the job, which can rob them of their acumen, judgement, perspective and drive. In one company, I was given a tip to inspect the women's washrooms after work for evidence of drug use. Sure enough, I found small torn packages containing remnants of white powder by the side of the sink. I was never able to prove who the user or users were, but I abhor this blatant use of drugs by employees on company premises. It is difficult enough to conduct a turnaround with employees who are sharp and on their toes. One doesn't need the added problem of employees on drugs.

In the same company, I was suddenly made aware that large sums of petty cash were being taken out without authorization. Soon after that, considerably larger cheques were being cashed as bank drafts. After some digging into the affair, we discovered that a series of large cheques had been written and cashed by one of the front office clerks. The most appalling part of this embezzlement case was that the clerk had used one of my signed cheques to practise on. We actually discovered the cheque where the clerk had traced my name over and over, until he had the motion to his satisfaction, and had signed a fairly good likeness of my name to the many cheques he successfully cashed at the bank. Very little of the cash was actually recovered. In a company already desperate for cash, this loss did not make my job any easier.

The turnaround person must be prepared to discover theft and fraud, even among trusted employees. The controls on the writing of cheques and the issuing of cheques must be rigorous. All company cheques should be pre-numbered, and when issued they must be described in a register indicating the cheque number, the amount, the date and the name of the payee. The register must show the initials of a senior officer of the company beside the cheque description, before the cheque can be issued. And no cheque should be issued without at least two signatures. These are the minimum precautions that a turnaround person should insist upon.

It is not only the employees who can play strange games. In one instance where I was asked to examine a company in trouble, I quickly discovered that the owner was implicated in a scheme which benefitted a member of his family, to the detriment of his own company. It turned out that his son owned a company which used one of his father's products as a raw material. The son purchased the raw materials, but never paid for them. These purchases remained on the books of the father's company as overdue accounts receivable, which went back for years. Obviously, one of the father's company's problems was the fact that a portion of his receivables were not being collected. His son's company, meanwhile, was obtaining free raw materials. Since it must have been quite obvious to the owner what the problem was, I never did figure out what to do to correct the situation, and I abandoned the contract.

The human side of the company is the most complex, the most difficult to assess, and the most difficult to fix. Sometimes, the wisest course of action for the turnaround person is to change the players, if this is possible. It this is not possible, retiring from the mandate may be the simplest solution.

7
Examining the Manufacturing Process & Measuring Productivity

I have always been amazed at how few companies actually measure productivity. And even when they do measure it, they do not necessarily use the information to their advantage. In one turnaround assignment, which involved a plastic film extrusion operation, the plant engineer generated a daily machine output sheet. This sheet clearly stated that their two 4.5-inch (11.5 cm) polyethylene mono-film extruders were generating typical outputs of 450 pounds (204 kg) per hour and 550 pounds (249 kg) per hour of film, respectively, at a particular thickness.

I had never been involved with plastic film extrusion, and therefore I didn't know whether these outputs were considered good or not. But a simple telephone call to the sales representative of the resin supplier quickly confirmed that a 4.5-inch (11.5 cm) polyethylene film extruder in new condition should be capable of an output of close to 1200 pounds (543.6 kg) per hour at the same thickness. True, as the barrel and the screw wore down through continuous use, and the tolerances became less precise, the machine would lose efficiency. But for a relatively small periodic investment in maintenance, the barrel and screw could be restored to their original condition. Carefully maintained charts would tell management how long the machine had been in service, how many pounds had been cumulatively produced by the machine, and what was the loss in efficiency over time. But to permit a machine to drop to less than 40% of its rated capacity, and worse still, not even appear to recognize the fact, is poor management. No wonder the company was in trouble!

Let us be clear on one point: machinery virtually never produces at its rated capacity. The manufacturer's ratings are always overstated, and are generated under absolutely ideal conditions. However, in the real world nothing is ever ideal. The power supply will probably fluctuate by plus or minus 5% depending upon location. The factory compressed air pressure will not be regulated to the optimum level. The factory air will contain some oil. The plant temperature will be warmer than ideal, and even moderate use will cause wear on the working parts, creating gear backlash and over-sized clearances. Then there are always losses through heat and friction. In my experience, any machinery operating at better than 92% of its rated capacity may be considered as excellent performance.

Maintenance

Of course, there are the ever present mechanical or electrical breakdowns, which inevitably bite into productive time. Even in the most modern automated plant, where the machine schedules may not be dictated by humans, the necessary preventive maintenance programs and the occasional power failure will drop the machine efficiency to below optimum levels. It is extremely difficult to determine what "normal" down time should be for a given machine or group of machines.

Many years ago, when I was starting my career as a turnaround man, I was placed in charge of an ailing division of a large company. One evening as I sat in my office contemplating my next move, the president of the company, to whom I had never spoken before, came walking through the production department. He stopped in front of my office door, pointed to an old machine which wasn't operating, and asked curtly, "Why isn't that machine running?"

"Well, sir," I replied, "because it's ante-diluvian."

He said, "It's what?"

"It's from before the Great Flood, sir," I replied.

"What flood?" he shouted.

I realized the president was irritated, and didn't understand what I was talking about. So I explained, "Sir, it's old and it's broken."

The president straightened up to his full height, looked me straight in the eye, and bellowed, "Dammit, man, learn to schedule your breakdowns!" And with that, he turned on his heel and walked out. I have to admit that over the years I have had a good many chuckles over that incident, and try as I might, I have never learned the art of scheduling breakdowns.

Breakdowns, by their very nature, are unpredictable. Machinery fails for a variety of reasons such as stress cracking, wear, poor choice of lubricants, hostile ambient conditions, operator error and, in extreme cases, even sabotage. Electronic equipment, too, is not immune from the occasional breakdown, although components are far more reliable today than when they first were used in industrial settings. It was not too many years ago that an up-time figure of greater than 97% for an industrial computer was considered excellent performance. Today, 3% down-time would be a recipe for disaster.

Preventive maintenance (P/M) programs can help reduce maintenance down-time, but they require a great deal of detailed paperwork and clerical input. Regular oiling and greasing with the proper lubricants is a simple first step towards a good P/M program. The major oil company sales representatives and sales engineers can be extremely helpful in this regard. After that comes a detailed historical analysis of breakdowns, so that an effort can be made to identify which parts will be most likely to fail, together with their estimated time to failure. The measurement of bearing wear, gear backlash and other key factors can be of great assistance in predicting the failure of equipment. In this way, it is hoped that key parts will be replaced just before the end of their useful life. It is important to keep a stock of parts in inventory which might be difficult to obtain, or which have long order lead times.

The objective of a good and detailed P/M program is to reduce breakdown maintenance down-time by increasing planned maintenance down-time, until the optimum point on the down-time curve is reached. Of course, this must be balanced against the high cost to maintain a comprehensive P/M program. How much downtime is acceptable? There are probably no absolute answers, since maintenance requirements differ for every industry. For heavy machinery, I have always assumed in my budget calculations that annual maintenance costs including parts and labor of less than 5% of the replacement cost of the equipment can be considered reasonable.

Efficiency calculation

It is not necessarily the absolute efficiency figure which is important. There may not be any industry figures published against which to compare the company's performance. Sometimes it is very difficult to measure the plant's efficiency in simple terms. The operation may involve a complicated chemical process; or it may require a job-shop technique, where each job is tailor-made to a particular customer's specifications and cannot be compared to a standard. Not all processes are as clear-cut and as simple as extruding plastic film. It is doubtful that many competitors will know their total efficiency figures very accurately, and not many of these will be able to achieve better than average levels.

What is important is to know where the company's efficiency lies today, and compare it against what it was yesterday, or last week, or last month, or last year. The turnaround person must make the effort to identify some reasonably simple, easily calculated method of determining the efficiency of output. However, this may not be an easy matter. In its simplest terms, efficiency is measured as output over input. These outputs and inputs can be expressed in units of time, weight, dollars and so on, and might end up as pounds per hour, dollars per unit, man-hours per pound, direct labor dollars per sales dollar or something equally indicative of efficiency.

The turnaround person must very carefully devise a formula for calculating efficiency, so that only the net input is compared to the net output, whether pounds, hours, dollars or another unit of measurement is used. Several years ago I was involved in turning around a job-shop operation. They did not measure productivity, so I had to set about devising a calculation which would give me an indication of their progress. I hit upon the concept of sales per labor dollar, as a reasonable means of measuring productivity in a job-shop.

The calculation was complicated by the fact that some of the sales may have come directly from inventory, and therefore would not show labor-hours involved. Or some of the output may have been placed into inventory, and would not show up as sales. Therefore, the calculation had to account for output produced but not sold, as well as output sold but not produced inside that time frame. Furthermore, the material going into inventory or coming out of inventory was valued at Cost of Sales, which does not include administrative costs, selling expenses, development costs, financial expenses or profits. Sales, of course, were at fully loaded value.

The calculation was somewhat convoluted, but it gave me what I wanted, which was an indication of where the productivity stood relative to previous time periods. If there had been no improvement over time, then I knew that no progress had been made, even though I had no idea what the absolute value should have been. Nor did I know where the company stood relative to its competitors. At that moment, it didn't matter. The company was racing against itself.

The Measurement of Inefficiency

Another very important and often forgotten indicator is the measurement of the amount of product which is purchased as raw material, is processed and ends up not being sold. This category of raw material can be classified under three headings: scrap, waste and rework.

(1) Scrap

Scrap is normally the result of a production error. A hole might have been drilled in the wrong location; the hole might have been drilled too large or too long; a shaft might have been turned too thin; the wrong color might have been added to a batch; a heat-treatment stage might have been omitted; the dough might have been under-proofed, and so on. Often, these errors are the result of poor or insufficient supervision, inadequate training or the lack of clear instructions. Whatever the reason, scrap is extremely expensive for any company, and should be addressed by the turnaround person.

There may not be a simple way to determine the rate of scrap. It is sometimes necessary to measure or to weigh the theoretical materials required to produce the end products, and to estimate the scrap by comparing standard usage versus actual usage. It is helpful to determine the industry average, if the parameter can be obtained.

(2) Waste

Waste is a normal by-product of the production process. The material which is left over after a stamping operation; the chips created from a turning operation; the sludge at the bottom of a digester; it may be necessary to dispose of these unavoidable leftovers, although sometimes they can be re-processed and re-used. This disposal can be lucrative, if the waste material has a market value. Sometimes this waste is toxic or otherwise undesireable, and the company must pay to dispose of it. Either way, the expected waste should be accurately calculated and compared against a standard.

(3) Rework

There are instances when an end-product is not usable, and the materials can be down-graded and re-used in small quantities as a raw material. Plastic, for example, can be ground up, pelletized and re-used as a raw material provided the color of the new product is darker than the previous product. Although the raw material is not lost, the use of re-ground material is expensive. The cost of labor and manufacturing overheads required to process the same material for a second time can never be recovered. Furthermore, it can be assumed that any rework will denigrate the end product, and therefore the sales value may be reduced. The turnaround person must maintain a very close watch on re-grind inventories, if direct labor and manufacturing overheads are to be carefully controlled.

Many companies, even very large ones, are unaware of their waste, scrap or rework rates because they simply do not measure them. They have no procedures to compare the raw materials going into production with the acceptable product coming out, nor to compare the required labor against the actual labor for a given production quantity. During a tour of a large well-known telecommunications firm, I was taken through the department which produced printed circuit boards. These boards are extremely complex, and are rigorously tested solder-joint by solder-joint to ensure proper functioning. I asked our tour guide, who was the department process engineer, what the current rework rate was. He didn't know.

In fact, there may not be any easy way to accurately measure these quantities. But "quick and dirty" is better than nothing at all, and the turnaround person must devise some practical way to determine the magnitude of the losses and the inefficiencies, and to track them week-to-week or month-to-month.

Insidious time losses

Other ways by which a company can lose efficiency is through employee lost time and through the ineffective use of employee time. The most common single factors are absenteeism, accidents, union grievances and unnessary overtime.

(1) Absenteeism

In the ideal world, every employee should love his job, and will always make every effort to be at work on time, will never miss a day, and will always put in a full day's work. In fact, there are many happy, well-adjusted employees in this world, who do indeed love what they do, and who give their best for their company.

However, many turnaround situations are exacerbated by poor worker habits and attitudes, and in many cases the company's predicament causes employee morale to slip. The end result is often that absenteeism rises. The workers may be responding to their union's dictates, or may simply be expressing their own dissatisfaction with the status quo, but management notices a decided increase in Friday and Monday absenteeism, or a rash of calling in sick, or even a marked increase in mysterious back aches. It has been my experience that the labor force never runs out of "friendly" doctors who will side with the employee no matter how suspicious the ailment, and who will freely prescribe a week to ten days' rest off the job as part of the cure. Inevitably, the employee's absence will cause difficulty for the company, which has to find a capable replacement, train the replacement and fit the replacement employee into a temporary pay classification as interpreted by the labor contract. This disruption is expensive to any company, especially if it occurs repeatedly. If the absenteeism is truly caused by a "lost time" accident, this becomes doubly expensive for the company because its accident insurance premiums skyrocket if the accident rate jumps into a higher insurance bracket.

The turnaround person must face this problem head on, if the company's labor efficiency is to improve. Unfortunately, in a turnaround situation there may not be the time nor the money available to hire an industrial psychologist to determine the causes of the employee malaise. Very often, the turnaround person will have to take the bull by the horns, and organize myriad meetings with small groups of workers, to explain to them what the turnaround expert's role in the organization is, and where he or she thinks the company is going. Then he or she must elicit from the employees what their feelings are: their pet peeves about the company, their personal ambitions, where they want the company to be in the future, and to verbally express their place and role in it. In this way, the turnaround person can only hope to slowly instill positive feelings in the workforce, to gain the workers' confidence, and to cause them to believe in the company and its future. It can be done. But the job is tedious, and will take up a major portion of the turnaround person's time.

There are other, more direct steps that can be taken to attack specific aspects of absenteeism, such as the Monday or Friday syndrome. Clauses can be written into the labor agreement stating that a worker will not be paid for or credited with his sick day or the statutory holiday, unless he can provide a doctor's certificate showing adequate proof of illness. It has become commonplace for companies to pay the workers the equivalent of their sick day allowance in the form of wages, for each sick day not used, as an incentive to the employee not to call in sick. However, many of these incentive techniques may have to be negotiated into a labor contract, and in a turnaround situation there is usually not the time.

Furthermore, the person in charge of the turnaround must resist the temptation to re-open an existing labor contract in order to re-negotiate certain clauses or to insert new clauses. Re-opening a labor contract can lead to disaster, as the union leadership may see this as a two-way street, and may insist upon re-negotiating wage and other clauses which might be in their interest. The best the turnaround person can do is to make note of the specific changes which it would be advantageous to negotiate into the next labor agreement, and hold off until then.

(2) Grievances

In a unionized company, one of the simplest ways to determine whether the union relationship with management is healthy or not is by counting the active grievances. As the relationship deteriorates, as it often does when a company's financial fortunes are falling, the union tends to express its displeasure and frustration by filing innumerable grievances over even the most petty infraction or perceived infraction. This is done to annoy management, and to let management know loudly and clearly that it is not managing properly.

If the turnaround person is able to meet with the union leadership and explain his or her presence and purpose in the company, and if the confidence of the union leadership can be obtained, only then can the healing process begin at the worker level. Generally, responsible union leadership is willing to give the turnaround a chance to take hold, and will agree to a moratorium on the grievances. Sometimes it will insist on settling at least the major ones before letting the minor ones go. Again, it is up to the turnaround person to set the climate, and to make the first move toward the union. Even when a company is not unionized, there usually exists an informal and unaffiliated shop union with which one can deal and negotiate.

(3) Overtime

One of the obvious wastes of manpower and money is the use of overtime. In companies which work around the clock, or which operate on a multi-shift basis, overtime is usually limited. Shift workers rarely work overtime unless their relief does not show up, in which case the unfortunate worker is asked to extend his working hours until a relief worker is located.

In some union contracts, any work performed on a weekend is eligible for overtime premiums, even if the weekend forms an integral part of the workers' five day work week. Some contracts recognize a fourth shift, which can work over the weekend as a matter of course, without being eligible for overtime. These situations are simply the result of past negotiations, and there is little that a turnaround person can do in the short term to alter the situation.

There is the inevitable overtime claimed by the day workers: those who work typically from 8:00 a.m. to 4:30 p.m. with an unpaid half-hour off for lunch. It is these workers who can abuse the overtime privilege. For example, a worker can arrive to work late. Straight time pay will be docked for the time missed. However, he or she will probably be required to work overtime to make up the lost time, for which an overtime premium will be claimed. This ruse is surprisingly common.

A small amount of overtime is healthy, and if the overtime is fairly distributed so that all workers have an equal chance to take home some extra pay, then both the company and the workers can benefit from a little overtime. The optimum amount of overtime can be calculated. Depending upon whether the overtime is paid at time-and-one-half, double time or triple time, this labor cost can be weighed against the cost of hiring workers for full shifts at straight time.

If a company pays out no overtime, then it is not unreasonable to assume that there are too many people in the work-force, and the work load is too little to fill the labor hours available. In my experience, if the overtime premium hovers between 3% and 5% of the labor cost, then the labor force is probably about right. There is just a bit more work than there are persons to carry it out. When the overtime premium payments exceed these levels, and inch their way up around 8% or higher, then this should act as a warning flag to the turnaround person that too many labor dollars are being paid out in the form of overtime premiums.

Workers can, to some extent, influence the overtime. If management and labor supervision are inexperienced, or simply lax, then workers can slow their work pace so that they will be required to work overtime simply to get the required work done on time. This tactic is often used prior to labor negotiations, or when the work backlog is beginning to drop, as it often does in a troubled company. The turnaround person must be prepared to determine, usually with the help of an experienced and trusted production manager, whether the work pace is normal or whether the workers are slowing down to extend their backlog of work, or to obtain extra overtime premiums to supplement their pay checks. Periodic arbitrary measurements such as Direct Labor Hours per Sales Dollar can help the turnaround person determine, on a comparative basis, whether the labor efficiency is getting better or worse, and whether overtime is justified.

Worker efficiency

The human side of the equation is no better. Operators will stop the machine for a smoke break, or will cease feeding the machine temporarily while they discuss the latest hockey scores with a buddy, or will stop the machine a few minutes earlier than they should to get ready for lunch break. Not to mention absenteeism, union activity, late arrival and medical problems, real or imagined.

It is my experience that total machine efficiency above 87% can be considered above average, where "total machine efficiency" is defined as machine up-hours divided by total available hours. Depending upon how many shifts per day the machine is operated, the typical total available hours might be 8, 16 or 24 per day for the number of days per week the plant is open.

Labor costs

To make matters worse the company may have, over the years, negotiated labor agreements which gave the hourly workers pay increases which bore no relationship to the real cost of living increases, or which did not consider the increases of competitive companies. The result may be that the turnaround person may be faced with a workforce that is paid in excess of anything which could be considered reasonable under the circumstances. In fact, labor costs may be one reason why the company is in financial difficulty.

Data on the average pay scales for industry types and for specific geographic regions is generally available from local Chambers of Commerce. Very often it is possible to obtain copies of collective agreements from companies in the area, and even from direct competitors, if the Personnel Directors are friendly with each other.

In such cases, the choices are limited. The turnaround person may approach the labor body representatives or the union leaders, and propose an across-the-board pay cut. However, unless the workers believe that the company's financial troubles are not simply a ruse dreamed up by management to reduce wages, and unless the workers see that the management group is also being asked to cut its take-home pay, the likelihood of success at reducing workers' pay is small.

Conclusion

At this point, the turnaround manager will have completed the analysis, and will have determined the major causes of the company's difficulties. This can generally be completed inside of the first two to three weeks of the mandate. The turnaround manager must now be prepared to determine exactly how to implement the necessary changes. It is customary to prepare a written report stating the problems and the proposed action plan within the first four weeks of the mandate.

Part Two

Executing the Turnaround

Preparing the
Groundwork

Once the diagnostic stage has been completed, and the turnaround person feels sufficiently comfortable that he or she has a firm grasp on the problems, and a good understanding of the strengths and weaknesses of the key managers, everything is then ready to begin putting in place the building blocks that will pave the way for a lasting turnaround.

Attempting to Enforce Change

No matter what direction the turnaround person may think best for a troubled company, it is axiomatic that the employees must accept the new direction. The easiest group to convince should be top management, or certainly the board of directors, since these are the groups which normally hire the turnaround person to effect the necessary changes to the corporate culture and to the corporate direction. Although I did encounter surprising difficulty trying to convince one company president to make what I considered to be some obvious reductions in staffing levels, in general the managerial and clerical staffs are the easiest to deal with. The most difficult group to convince, in my experience, is the hourly-paid workforce.

The fact that a company's cash flow position is deteriorating cannot be kept a secret from the employees for very long. Concerned comments from the accounting staff, worried behavior of middle managers, cancellation of salary increases, complaints by suppliers about the slowness to pay – these things become known at all levels of an organization. Everyone soon knows that "the company is in trouble."

In a company where the office staff or the supervisors are not unionized, it is likely that these groups will suffer first from the lack of salary increases. The unionized workers have a signed contract, and no matter what, their increases will go through. Supervisors are goaded by their employees to unionize, so that they, too, can be guaranteed increases. Loyalties begin to shift, and employee morale starts to slip noticeably.

In the company which I described earlier, where the supervisors were told to stay in their offices, the workers knew that the union ran the company, and therefore they looked to the union leaders for guidance and leadership instead of to their supervisors and managers. It was extremely difficult to break the hold that the union had on the workers. I spent a long time holding structured meetings with small groups of employees, asking them what they liked or disliked about the company, what they wanted the company to be, how they saw their futures inside the company, and trying to get them to develop a positive image of the company. We listened to their complaints, and took positive action to correct those problems that we could within our limited budget. Slowly, the employees began to see that the new management meant to change things for the better, and a limited loyalty shift from the union to management became evident. Eventually, there was indeed a small but measurable increase in productivity. These cultural changes take a long time to effect, and I have no idea whether our efforts bore fruit in the long run.

Sometimes the results of the feelings towards the "new order" are immediately known. In one large company, the maintenance workers were unhappy with my choice of the maintenance manager, because evidently the new manager wanted his employees to account for their time on the job, something which had never been demanded of them before. I was called into the maintenance yard, because the employees were refusing to work. I can assure you that standing on a tool crate, surrounded by 150 angry men with wrenches in their hands, is not a pleasant experience.

One cannot make the mistake of bargaining with the union under duress, because the points that are conceded may have important repercussions for any future negotiations. Besides, if the turnaround person bargains in this manner and gives in on a point, then every time the employees feel angry about something they will simply refuse to work and call for the turnaround specialist to solve their problem. This action not only undermines the labor relations staff and renders them ineffectual, it becomes totally unproductive for the turnaround person, who will be working mainly to solve union disputes instead of doing more important things to turn the company's fortunes around.

On one occasion, a particularly difficult turnaround, it happened that the company was headed for a strike. The union had been subjected to a particularly patronizing management regime for many years, and the members wanted to vent all their antagonistic feelings against the company. The strike turned out to be a long and nasty one, marred by incidents of violence and destructive behavior. Supervisors' homes were targets of violence, company property was destroyed and anti-company feelings ran high. Pickets barred the entry of management personnel to the premises, and we had to open temporary offices at a remote location.

The union was convinced that I had been hired as a strike breaker, and I was not well liked by the union leaders. During the strike, several customers called and demanded that we return their parts which were in our shop for overhaul, repaired or not. The company owner had gone away on a holiday, leaving me in charge. Since I was the senior person, it was my responsibility to call the bailiff to obtain a court order to enter the plant and take out the parts for the customer. Each time we had to enter the premises, the bailiff had to call the police riot squad, who formed two lines of fully helmeted and armed men, through which the bailiff and I walked to gain entry to the plant.

As if by magic, a large group of strikers would begin to materialize behind the policemen, carrying baseball bats, shouting taunts and asking me to step outside the police lines, because they wanted to "talk" to me. The scene was repeated several times over a period of many weeks, and it was an extremely uncomfortable feeling to have to work under those conditions.

Turnarounds are not always fun. They have their trying moments. The turnaround person will be tested time and time again by the employees at all levels. It is part of the turnaround job, and must be balanced against the satisfaction of successfully restoring a company to health.

Cash Flow Projections

During a turnaround, it is mandatory for the financial manager to put out a cash flow projection every week. Not only will the bank manager want to know what the up-coming cash position will be, but the turnaround person will be able to take appropriate action on the basis of anticipated cash flows. Knowledge of expected inventory and receivables levels are also vital for the purposes of anticipating the line of credit which will be available to the company in the coming weeks.

It is normal for the turnaround person to experience resistance to the request for regular cash flow projections. Because the sales figures and the cash receipts are virtually impossible to know accurately, the exercise is really only an educated guess. But presumably someone in the sales or accounting staff knows which customers are fast payers, and which ones will accept a discount in return for fast payment. And someone in the marketing or sales departments must be able to provide a reasonable estimate of the immediate sales expectations. And there must be someone in the production department who can predict which shipments will go out within the next 30 days, and perhaps even provide a weekly shipment schedule. Granted, these figures are "best guesses," but they will be infinitely better than no guesses at all, and will become more accurate with time.

The expense side of the cash flow report is easier to determine, and the accounting staff will have an excellent grasp of the outgoing cash requirements of the company. The changes in manning levels, purchasing policies, accounts payable policies and other areas, which the person in charge of the turnaround has placed into effect, are relatively easily worked into the cash flow analysis. A turnaround manager without cash flow projections is like a driver on the highway without a road map. Typical long term and short term cash flow projection formats are shown in Figures 12 and 13.

Figure 12: A Comprehensive Long Term Cash Flow Projection

	Month 1	complete for each month of the year	Total Year 1

CASH IN:

Cash from Sales
Investor Input
R & D Credits
Long Term Loan
Sale of Assets

TOTAL CASH IN:

CASH OUT:

Capital Expenditures
Direct Labor inc. fringes

Raw Materials – Sales
Raw Materials – Inventory
Manufacturing Overheads

Selling Expenses
Administrative Expenses
Development Expenses

Financial Expenses
Loan Repayment
Dividends
Income Taxes

Less: Amortization & Depreciation

TOTAL CASH OUT:

NET CASH FLOW:

BANK POSITION   Initial =

Figure 13: A Typical Weekly Cash Flow Forecast

	Week 1	Week 2	Week 3	Week 4	Week 5	Week 6
CASH IN:						
Cash from Previous Shipments						
Cash from Forecast Shipments						
Other Cash Input						
TOTAL CASH IN:						
CASH OUT:						
Cheques in the Float						
Post-Dated Cheques						
Wages						
Salaries						
Commissions						
Fees						
Materials						
Supplies						
Sub-Contracts						
Utilities						
Phone & Fax						
Office Supplies						
Insurance						
Rent						
Transportation						
Promotional Materials						
Automotive						
Travel						
Legal Fees						
Audit Fees						
Loan Repayments						
Interest						
Lease						
Taxes						
Royalties						
Other						
TOTAL CASH OUT:						
CASH FLOW:						
BANK POSITION Initial =						

Sales, Operating and Capital Expense Budgets

Most line managers hate budgeting time. Nevertheless, the budgeting process is one of the most important tasks that any company faces, and all too often the smaller companies fail to produce annual budgets. The budget is the road map, and without it the management has no clear idea what the targets are, and what is considered acceptable performance. Budgets may be fixed, which means that they are insensitive to the sales levels, or they may be flexible, and vary with fluctuating sales levels. Irrespective of the type of budgeting process, the fact remains that a company must have detailed budgets if it is to survive.

It is one of the tasks of the turnaround person to determine that the existing budgets are reasonable, realistic and achievable. If no budgets exist in the company, then the turnaround manager must see to it that appropriate budgets are prepared, post-haste.

The sales budget must reflect sales levels which the sales force considers achievable, and should indicate a breakdown by product line, by salesman and by territory, so that all salesmen can fully understand what is expected of them. The sales budget should reflect any seasonal nature of the product, and should take into account a realistic timetable to cover the introduction of a new product or product line.

All too often, the turnaround person is being pressured by the bank or by other lending institutions with loans in the company, to show a rapid recovery. The temptation is to exaggerate the sales growth so that these lenders will be satisfied for the moment, and reduce some of the pressure. Unfortunately, the reality of the situation always catches up with one's efforts, and in my experience it is better to aim low and exceed expectations, than it is to aim high and appear to have failed.

Operating budgets are probably the simplest budgets to develop, because there are so many known and fixed factors involved in the operations. To be sure, some items are variable and directly dependent upon sales levels. But for the most part, the line item costs can be readily identified. Once the sales budgets are in place and the hourly-paid staffing levels are determined, and the management structure is established, the operating budget should be completed relatively quickly.

Figure 14: A Sample Discounted Cash Flow Analysis

Example: A company is contemplating the purchase of a machine to increase output by 1 000 units per month. It is estimated that this additional output will increase annual revenues by $18 000 in the first year, and $20 000 thereafter.

The machine will cost $30 000, and will cost an additional $5 000 to install and start up.

The estimated useful life of the machine is estimated to be 5 years, and the scrap or resale value has been set at $5 000. The investment recovery time is assumed to equal the useful life of the equipment, or 5 years.

To calculate the Rate of Return (ROI) on the investment, determine the correct discount rate that will cause the net cash flow to equal zero. The ROI is calculated to be 18%.

Year	0	1	2	3	4	5
Purchase Price	-30 000					
Installation	-5 000					
Increased Revenue		18 000	20 000	20 000	20 000	20 000
Cost of raw mat'ls.		-6 000	-6 000	-6 000	-6 000	-6 000
Increased dir. labor		-1 500	-1 500	-1 500	-1 500	-1 500
Increased O/H & Exp.		-1 000	-1 000	-1 000	-1 000	-1 000
Resale Value						5 000
Net Cash Flow	-35 000	9 500	11 300	11 000	10 700	15 200
Discount Rate=18.0%						
Discount Factor from present value tables.	1.000	0.847	0.718	0.609	0.516	0.437
Discounted Cash Flow	-35 000	8 047	8 113	6 669	5 521	6 642
Cumulative Discounted Cash Flow	-35 000	-26 953	-18 840	-12 141	-6 620	22

There should be a carefully documented capital expenditure budget, showing exactly what equipment is required and what it is required for. When a capital expenditure is being contemplated, the requesting manager should be required to prepare a Return on Investment (ROI) calculation, in order to justify the purchase. The preferred method of ROI calculation is the Discounted Cash Flow method, which will indicate the relative degree by which the proposed expenditure would be better than simply putting the money into the bank, or investing it in the bond market. A brief description of the Discounted Cash Flow calculation method is shown in Figure 14.

It is generally considered good practice to allow managers to substitute equipment items not in the budget for those which are in the budget, so as not to exceed the total amount in the budget. However, the turnaround person may decide, in view of the tight financial position of the company, not to permit any but the absolutely necessary capital acquisitions. For example, those required for employee safety, or those required to replace non-functioning essential equipment.

Expediting and Scheduling

In one company in which I was responsible to effect a turnaround, I discovered to my horror that we were late in over 35% of all customers' orders. There were a multitude of reasons why this was so, starting with late delivery of raw materials, and continuing with the fact that there was little scheduling of individual orders through the shop. There were no expediters assigned to individual orders, so they were completed whenever the supervisors involved got around to it. I further realized that those orders which were more difficult to complete were shunted to the back of the queue, in order to allow the easier orders through.

In another company desperately in need of a turnaround, I discovered to my amazement that there was no scheduling of orders through the manufacturing process. It was left to the discretion of the individual supervisors to push the orders through, and as might be expected, late orders were pushed through on the basis of which salesman could scream the loudest.

There are no packaged answers for the performance of the scheduling and expediting functions in a manufacturing environment. Each situation requires its own solutions. However, it should be obvious that if a company is to survive in a competitive environment, the turnaround person will have to devote some time to these extremely important areas. Obviously, the target of zero late orders may be achievable only at great expense, and the turnaround person will have to evaluate the cost of perfection versus the cost of practicality.

The decision to establish a scheduling department, or to institute the position of expediters, will depend upon the size of the company and the ability to absorb these overheads. But the necessity to properly service customers with on-time deliveries is extremely important.

It is equally important that inventory be tightly controlled in a company that manufactures commodity items, or manufactures for inventory in advance of anticipated sales. It is always the tendency of salespersons to want to have more than enough inventory on hand, in case of sudden customer demand. This inventory is expensive to hold, just in case it is needed. The turnaround person will have to provide guidance to the scheduling department regarding inventory levels, to balance inventory holding costs against the lost-opportunity cost of stock-outs. This is truly like walking a tight-rope, and it is difficult to strike an ideal balance.

Purchasing

It is an important duty of the person in charge of a turnaround to ensure that the purchasing function is carried out by competent and qualified persons. The guidelines for the purchasing function should be clearly spelled out, such as the number of quotations required before placing an order, the duration and limits of a blanket purchase agreement, economic re-order quantities, inventory re-order points, taking into account the delivery lead-times of the material, and splitting raw-materials purchases among at least two suppliers, in case of the failure of a major supplier.

Every buyer is faced with a dilemma whenever a volume discount is offered. Should the discount be accepted and a larger quantity of material be purchased than the company can realistically use up inside a normal time period? There are simple formulae which can be applied to such situations, utilizing the cost of money over time, and the purchaser can be trained to calculate the breakeven point between the savings of a volume discount versus the cost of holding inventory. It is generally a good policy to restrict the purchasing power of an individual buyer to a limited dollar value, above which the purchase order would have to be signed by a higher authority.

It is possible that the cash shortage suffered by the company in need of a turnaround is so severe that it may have soured the relationship between the company and many of its suppliers. Some suppliers may be so upset at not having been paid for 180 days or more that they will adamantly refuse to sell to the company. In such cases it is imperative that the buyers have a wide knowledge of alternative suppliers, and that they develop their network of alternative suppliers as quickly as possible.

It is probable that a new supplier will want to receive a credit rating on the company, prior to shipping materials. Companies with cash flow problems do not have good credit ratings. Therefore, it is an old trick that a company in a turnaround mode should always maintain one or two suppliers fully paid up on a 30-day basis, who can be utilized as credit references. However, these tricks do not fool the credit agencies, only a few unsuspecting suppliers.

In many turnaround situations, the buyer has no choice but to purchase minimum quantities of stock on a Cash-Before-Delivery (CBD) basis. This situation is frustrating for a professional buyer, but circumstances may not permit otherwise. Nevertheless, the turnaround manager should establish the ground-rules for the buyers in the event that the company's financial situation changes for the better. It is too easily forgotten that a good purchaser can save the company money through careful buying practices, and that a savings of only 1% on purchases of $10 million is $100 000, which could well become the difference between a profit and a loss.

In the plastic extrusion company mentioned previously, we finally reached the sales volume where it made sense to negotiate car-load volumes of resin with our major supplier. I had negotiated what I considered to be an excellent deal for receiving resin by the car-load, and I anxiously awaited delivery of the first rail car. It finally arrived, and we had it shunted onto our siding close to the raw material silo, in preparation for unloading the following morning.

The plant was located in one of the city's tougher neighborhoods. As it happened, some enterprising people, looking for excitement, grabbed several wooden pallets which they found nearby, and built a bonfire under the belly of the rail car, causing all the resin to melt inside the car. When I arrived the next morning, the resin had solidified into a solid mass inside the car, and I had to send the car back to the supplier in unusable condition. I don't know who was more upset, the supplier or me. So much for carefully laid plans.

Quality Assurance

In this world of increasing competitiveness, many customers are quickly becoming accustomed to improved product quality standards. The turnaround person may be faced with a situation that calls for unusually high Quality Assurance standards which require adherence to Military Specifications. Nomenclatures such as Z-299.4/3/2/1, ISO-9003/2/1, and AQAP-9/4/1 might appear as mandatory Quality Assurance requirements, and the turnaround person may be totally unfamiliar with these terms.

Large companies such as General Motors, General Electric, Alcan, Dominion Engineering, Bell Telephone and many others are increasingly insistent that their suppliers comply with certain designated levels of Quality Assurance. This insures that their own products will be of high quality and will meet the requirements set by state regulatory bodies. More and more small companies, wishing to become suppliers to these giants, are being forced to comply with quality standards never before considered necessary.

Under the terms of a recognized Quality Assurance program, there are very strict rules regarding the treatment of product as it flows through the factory, with respect to the inspection of the goods, handling of inspection equipment, and the traceability of each lot or batch as it is produced. The company's accreditation with the Quality Management Institute (QMI) is dependent upon the company's compliance with strict rules of conduct, and periodic audits by the QMI determine whether accreditation will be lost or maintained.

The rules under which a Quality Assurance program are operated are complex, and may be bewildering to a turnaround person who has never worked under these strict conditions. Nevertheless, the person in charge of a turnaround may be faced with the necessity to implement quality standards which conform to specific accreditation designations. These quality assurance programs typically add between 15% and 25% to a company's operating overheads, and the advantages and drawbacks of a quality assurance program must be very carefully considered prior to implementation.

Earlier in my career, when I began a turnaround assignment for a company involved in the manufacture of aircraft components, we received an inquiry from a British aircraft company. The Telex ended with the statement: "Subject to the usual B.S." Understandably, this statement caused the inevitable guffaws and gales of laughter in the office, until an older and experienced fellow worker explained to us that this stood for: "Subject to the usual British Standards."

APPENDIX III describes in detail the concepts of a Quality Assurance program designed to meet the requirements of Z 299.2, ISO 9002, and AQAP-4. These represent a minimum aerospace standard in the Western world, but many companies will be able to operate under less stringent requirements. Nevertheless, the principles are the same, irrespective of the accreditation level, and are important to understand.

Determining the Proper Marketing Strategy

One of the most fundamental questions that must be asked is, "how much damage has the company name suffered in the market place?" Non-payment of invoices, and the inability to service customers promptly because of a lack of cash to pay for raw materials, will quickly destroy a company's reputation in the market place.

Companies in financial difficulty generally lose orders because they cannot find sufficient suppliers who will sell them raw materials except on a CBD (cash before delivery) basis. Often all sources of supply have been exhausted, all suppliers of services have been burned, and there is nowhere left to turn. This inability to obtain materials and supplies as required will have an important effect upon the company's ability to service its customers quickly and effectively. Hence, the sales and accounting functions are inextricably intertwined, and must work closely with each other in order to rebuild the company's former position, and regain credibility in the marketplace.

Talking to Suppliers

The inability to pay an invoice on time is an embarassing state of affairs, and most Accounts Payable clerks have difficulty on the telephone when confronted by an angry supplier who demands payment. Even Chief Accountants feel embarrassment when they must skate and dance around the simple fact that they just don't have the funds in the bank to pay an invoice, even if it is only a matter of a few hundred dollars.

The common thing to do is to simply avoid the subject altogether, and not call the irate suppliers. This absence of comment from the delinquent company only serves to further anger the suppliers, who are by now convinced that you are trying to avoid them. Suppliers who are owed money for long periods of time, and who are ignored by the one who owes the money, often become very aggressive and nasty. It only takes three creditors to place a company into formal receivership, and it is a fallacy to believe that a creditor who is only owed a few hundred dollars will not pursue a debtor. I have known creditors to place a company into bankruptcy for amounts of only a few hundred dollars, simply because they are angry and feel vindictive.

It is therefore extremely important that the person in charge of the turnaround impose a policy of contacting creditors. A creditor's call must be returned. If an invoice cannot be paid, do not lie and tell the creditor that the cheque is in the mail, or that it will be sent to him on Friday, or any other excuse to get rid of the caller. Explain the situation carefully, and try to find a few dollars to pay a part of what is owed, even if the amount is pitifully small. Surprisingly, a creditor's patience can be expanded remarkably if an effort is made to remain open and honest. It seems that most people and companies have suffered through hard times at one time or another, and more often than not the person at the other end of the phone will be far more understanding of your situation than you would expect.

Of course, there will always be exceptions to this rule, and some creditors seem to have hearts of ice. These people must be dealt with firmly, and told that they will be paid when the money is available.

Re-establishing Credit

If the turnaround efforts are successful, and the cash flow is beginning to normalize, one of the more difficult tasks of the delinquent company is to re-establish reasonable payment terms and a realistic line of credit with its suppliers.

In most cases, normalizing terms of payment is a matter of time, so that the suppliers can have a chance to observe the delinquent company, and determine that it is indeed coming out of its problems. It will be impossible for suppliers to run a credit check, because presumably all suppliers are on a COD or CBD basis. But all reasonable suppliers would like to resume normal business relations with a delinquent company, for two reasons: first, because it gives them a chance to recover what is owed; and second, in hard times it is not easy to find replacement customers, and after all, business is business.

The turnaround person can play an important role in re-establishing normalized relations with suppliers. Personal visits to the supplier's premises, with an explanation of what happened, and a description of what has been done to rectify the situation, will go a long way to alleviate the supplier's doubts, and re-build much-needed credibility.

Visiting Customers

Salespersons quickly lose their morale when faced with hostile customers, and few things will irk customers more than late delivery and a lack of service. Troubled companies typically have difficulty servicing their clients properly, and customers will of necessity seek alternate sources of supply. Relationships with sales representatives rapidly deteriorate, and what may have been the result of years of effort on the part of a particular salesperson may evaporate in a matter of weeks.

All this goodwill can be extremely difficult to rebuild. The customer may have found not only an alternate source of supply, but one who offers better service, cheaper prices and who has an equally affable sales force. If the turnaround is to take effect, the turnaround person faces the prospect of having to re-establish contact with the customers, and to rebuild a climate of confidence among a reticent client base.

None of this should be done alone or in a vacuum. The turnaround expert must involve the person in charge of sales and marketing, and must always maintain close contact with the chief accountant, to ensure that the customer service levels are available, and that the cash will be on hand to provide the necessary materials, so that the credibility of the company is never undermined. It is also important that the person in charge of the turnaround effort be sensitive to the fact that many such visits to customers may be required, if the client base is to be saved.

Rebuilding the Sales Department

It is understood that the turnaround person has assessed the competence of the incumbent head of the marketing function, and has decided either to keep or replace that person. In any event, once the chosen head of marketing is in place, the turnaround manager's attention must now be turned to jointly developing a plan to rebuild customer confidence, customer service and sales levels. Sales territory allocation, distribution methods, merchandising policy, agents' fees, all these policies and more must be scrutinized, questioned and closely examined from the ground up. Should inventories be placed into customers' premises on consignment, should salespersons be assigned to particular customers, and how many on-the-road salespersons should there be, if at all?

One of the most effective ways to rebuild the salespersons' confidence and to focus the salespersons' efforts is to hold weekly meetings with all of the sales personnel. These meetings should be kept as short as possible, and should be directed specifically toward identifying sales prospects, identifying contacts, expressing problems and concerns, eliminating obstacles to closing sales, and allowing each salesperson the opportunity to tell the group what sales he or she closed during the past week.

It is extremely important for the sales manager to insist that the salespersons' commissions should always be tied to collected sales, and not booked sales, in order to avoid paying a commission for a sale which did not realize any revenues, either because the customer did not pay or because the merchandise was returned for some reason.

These meetings will, if properly handled, become a good-natured contest between the salespersons, to see who can close the most sales, or who can open the most new accounts. This rivalry is healthy, and is the best way to encourage the salespersons to give their utmost for the company. These meetings will also identify the strong salespersons, and will encourage the weaker ones to work harder to keep up.

Another important item which the head of Marketing must keep track of is the status of all quotations received. It is altogether too easy for individual salespersons to forget about quotation due dates, or to neglect filling out a request for quotation because the level of detail was too time consuming or too complicated. Indeed, many requests for quotation are extremely complex to fill out, and may be far above the ability of the average salesperson. Requests for quotations may well be the life-blood of a company's marketing efforts, and they must be carefully and continuously monitored. Too many companies lose important potential sales because quotations lie unanswered.

The role of the Inside salesperson at the order desk must also be well defined. The Inside sales position is important to the success of a company, because it is normally the first line of contact for customer inquiries. The Inside salesperson must be chosen for his or her voice personality, and must appear extremely knowledgeable about the company's product lines and its pricing policies. Training in these areas is vital. Ringing telephones should be answered promptly. The turnaround person should be sensitive to the importance of the personnel at the order desks in presenting the company personality to the outside world.

Measuring Product Costs

I am always struck by how few companies know the real cost of manufacturing their products. Whenever a sales representative complains that a competitor is offering a similar product at a price the company cannot match, the first thought that comes into my head is that the competitor does not know the product costs.

Product costing is not easy. It involves breaking down the operations into quantifiable portions, and defining the direct costs applicable to each portion. First, one must establish the direct labor and raw materials requirements, and a realistic allowance for scrap and rework, inefficiencies, and a determination of average output per unit time. If the manufacturing process is complex, it may be necessary to create convenient algorithms in order to simplify the costing process. In very complex manufacturing processes, some companies allocate costs, which might even include certain overheads, to specific machining centres.

Then one must allocate an appropriate overhead burden to the product or product line. The overheads are absorbed according to the sales forecasts, and if sales exceed forecast, then the overheads will become over-absorbed. Conversely, if sales fall short of forecast, then the overheads will be under-absorbed. It will become the responsibility of the accounting department to run periodic comparisons of estimated costs versus actual costs, so that the published product costs can be revised from time to time.

All of this effort is time consuming, and the end result is not guaranteed to be accurate. Nonetheless, the exercise of product costing is extremely important to the turnaround person, because he must know which products are "winners" and which are "losers." It is up to the person in charge of the turnaround to weed out unprofitable products or product lines, even though the exercise will without doubt reduce the overall sales potential.

Notwithstanding any attempts to weed out unprofitable product lines, it must be understood that sometimes one simply cannot discontinue products indiscriminately. It stands to reason that a full product line may comprise many styles, shapes, colors and sizes. It is also reasonable to assume that not all of the products inside a product line will be equally easy to manufacture, or that the cost of raw materials will be uniform across the product line.

The customer, on the other hand, might insist that small items inside the product line shall cost less than large items. Perhaps that is the way your competitors price their lines. Furthermore, customers may insist that the only way they will buy from you, is if you offer the whole product line. Thus, you may find yourself in the position where you are forced to sell a particular item at a loss, if you wish to continue to sell the product line. If the gross sales of the product line are profitable, then it can be considered a necessary evil to sell some items at a loss. It is important to maintain a close watch on the sales mix, to observe whether customers alter their buying habits to favor the unprofitable items.

Price Estimating

The price estimating function is closely related to the product costing function, and accurate estimates are impossible without accurate costs. Estimating is, in fact, the heart of the entire pricing function. It is extremely important for the turnaround person to understand in detail the estimating process of the company. The most obvious question which should be asked is whether all the cost factors are indeed being taken into account. And even if they are, are they indeed accurate? Particularly such nebulous factors as waste, scrap, production inefficiency, rework and shrinkage. Management generally does not like to admit to any degree of inefficiency, but if these factors are not carefully taken into account in the estimating function, the resultant estimates could be out as much as 10% or more.

Some companies attempt to allocate specific overheads to each product, and the estimating function can become a cumbersome effort, involving complicated calculations and allocations of arbitrary overhead figures. I favor a simple approach, where the direct costs are accounted for as accurately as possible, and then a target contribution percentage is assigned to the product to cover expenses, overheads and profit.

The person in charge of the estimating function will have to be carefully instructed as to what percent contribution to use in his or her calculations. The dilemma is simple to describe. A financially troubled company usually needs all the sales it can get, and the tendency is to keep the contribution requirement low, in order to win as many sales contracts as possible by offering the lowest bids. But lowering the bid price can mean that overheads are not sufficiently covered, and any hope of making a profit may be clearly wiped out. In the extreme case, the company may be "wrapping its products in dollar bills," and simply burrowing farther into the financial hole. There are no simple rules or answers to this dilemma, and the turnaround manager will have to use his or her judgement and experience to set the ground-rules for the estimating group.

Obtaining the Much-Needed Cash

It goes without saying that companies in financial difficulty experience a cash shortage. In most cases, if the problems have reached the stage where a turnaround person must be called in, these cash flow problems have probably reached catastrophic proportions. No invoices are being paid, creditors are telephoning constantly for their money, and both the president and the controller are having their calls carefully screened. Their secretaries are instructed to inform all callers that the president or the controller is out, and that the call will be returned as soon as he or she comes in. This survival scenario is played out thousands of times a day all over the industrial world, particularly during a recession.

In some cases, the employee cuts which the person in charge of the turnaround has effected both at the hourly paid worker level and at the management level, coupled with any project and capital expansion cuts, may have been sufficient to halt the negative cash flow. Or perhaps changes to the marketing philosophy effected by the turnaround person have sufficiently increased the sales so that incoming cash is now able to offset the negative cash flow. Unfortunately, however, these measures are not usually sufficient to reverse a negative cash flow in time to save a company. As soon as the lending institutions sense a problem, they quickly lose confidence in the company and in the management, and they will set a tight timetable for turnaround.

In most turnaround circumstances, the ailing company will require an infusion of working capital to maintain its operations, to purchase its raw materials (especially on a CBD basis), and to expand its sales efforts. There are several avenues open to a company in its search for funding, but all avenues will become dead-ends unless there are two important ingredients in place before proceeding. These are:

1. A clear vision of where the company wishes to be within the next two, three and five years, with a detailed strategy which outlines exactly how the company will achieve its goals and realize its vision.

2. A competent, proven and credible management team to execute the strategic plan.

Only with these two ingredients in place, does the turnaround have any real hope of being achieved.

The Vision

Describing how to establish a clear vision of where a company wishes to be at some definite time in the future is, of course, impossible in a book such as this. Each company is different, each set of circumstances is unlike any other, and no two people have identical visions of where they want to go, and how they intend to get there. However, the guiding principle is always to determine a set of circumstances which will place the company in a position of competitive advantage. The following are some useful questions which can be asked, which could act as guidelines to identifying company visions and strategies in general terms:

* It is always useful in a very competitive market to look at niche market positions. Does the company possess a particular product-line strength which the company could exploit to gain an advantage over its competition?

* Does the company have any particular strengths in its customer service policies or warranty policies or distributorships which it could exploit to gain a competitive advantage?

* Are there any particular technical strengths which the company could exploit to gain a competitive advantage? Or is there any super-modern fast equipment available which would place the company at the forefront of the industry?

* Are there any marketplace weaknesses that could be exploited? For example, if the manufacturers in the particular market segment are fragmented and weak,

would a policy of well planned mergers and acquisitions place the company at a competitive advantage?

* If the industry is in general considered "low-tech," is there any possibility of infusing medium- or high-technology into the industry, either through a strategic alliance with a technology-driven company, or through the inception of an innovative research & development program, to gain a competitive advantage?
* If the industry is mature, would a strategic acquisition in a related but distinct industry provide needed variation and stimulus to a stodgy product line?
* If the industry is "high-tech," would a strategic alliance with a related but non-competing line provide the needed stability in a volatile market place?

The Strategy

The strategy outlining the steps to achieve the vision must also be carefully thought out and committed to paper. Strategies can be as varied as the senior executive's imagination will permit, but all strategies must be designed with one goal in mind: how will the company achieve its short, medium and long term objectives? The following is a simple list of questions that might be asked when formulating a strategy for future direction:

* What corporate structure is best for the company, and how, when and by whom will the key positions be filled?
* What is the optimum sales and marketing structure for the company, and what would be the best service, quality, merchandising and distribution strategies?
* What capital acquisitions are required, and how will they be financed?
* What is the best capital/debt/financial structure for the company, and what steps must be taken to achieve it?
* What type of merger/acquisition policy would be in the best interest of the company, taking into consideration product-line compatibility, sales volume, foreign or domestic, state of the technology and financial status of the merger/acquisition target?

* What is the technology gap that must be crossed, and what steps must be taken to bridge the gap?
* Which product lines (or operating divisions) should be dropped or added, to improve profitability or to complete the company's range of products and services, or to best fit its targeted market?

The Shell Game

The strategy in the case of a privately held company may include taking the company public. This may be a viable way of bringing in much needed cash. This strategy involves purchasing a "shell," an existing but dormant company which is listed on a stock exchange. Generally, these shells are the remains of no-longer operating companies whose shares are not actively traded, and are worth a few pennies at best. Such shells are found on the more adventuresome stock exchanges which are known for their non-risk-averse policies. There are many accounting and legal firms whose partners are aware of the availability of shell companies, and some are indeed experts in the practice of locating and acquiring shells.

The important part of acquiring a shell company is to find one that is "clean," that is to say, a shell without a lawsuit hanging over it, and without angry creditors ready to take action at the first signs of re-birth. The purchase price for a clean shell does not come cheaply, and when all the legal and accounting fees are added in, the price can easily exceed $150 000. The private company is then merged into the shell company, thus becoming a public company. The legal and accounting experts who carried out the process will generally retain some portion of the shares for their efforts.

If a friendly investment dealer has been identified at the outset and is able to sell a portion of the shares held by the public company on the open market, then this sale of shares can yield considerable sums of cash. The potential market value of the shares can in some cases add up to several million dollars. Then the experienced administrator can, through well-timed press releases indicating company progress, new product launches, research and development breakthroughs, sales increases and other good news, influence the stock price steadily upward. This is not a strategy for the faint of heart, and is best left to experts with considerable experience.

The Management Team

No investors, whether they are private or institutional, will invest important sums in a company where the management team has not impressed them as being competent, experienced and possessing a proven track record. One of the primary tasks of the turnaround person is to ensure that the best available managers that the budget can afford are put into the key senior positions. That is not to say that all positions must be filled with persons from outside the company. On the contrary, overlooking talent from within can be detrimental to employee morale. Wherever it can be found, be it from inside or from outside the company, it is important that it be the best available for the price affordable.

There is also a myth, which still has a surprising number of adherents, that a senior manager must come from the industry. "One has to be a baker to run a bakery." Obviously, they say, someone from the "outside" does not carry the knowledge to successfully handle the challenge of a new job. While it is true that someone from outside a particular industry must learn certain facts and peculiarities about a new industry, it is equally true that this person will not bring to the new job all the negative baggage, closed-mindedness, conservative behaviors and entrenched attitudes of the former industry. Sometimes a fresh approach can be invaluable.

One cannot over-emphasize the importance of the management team in a turnaround situation. In one instance where I had been entrusted with the turnaround of a small company, the owner was the life-blood of the company. He was the key to the future success of the turnaround effort. He had personally developed each of the major clients, he knew each contact personally, and he was responsible for the technological success of the product line. In addition, he was a remarkably good salesman. He was, however, a weak administrator, and had gone bankrupt twice before. This was the third time the lending bank was witnessing his company going under. The bankers had no confidence in the man, and they were not going to support me or the company, no matter how good the turnaround plan was, so long as the owner remained in the business. Without the owner, there was no business. With the owner, there was no investor. A "catch-22" situation if ever there was one!

In this particular situation, the accepted solution was to bring in additional investors who would dilute the original owner's equity to a position of less than 50%. Both the lending bank and the original owner accepted this compromise.

Once a competent management team is in place, the turnaround person will have to work closely with the team to set out clearly the milestones and targets for sales levels, production efficiency and profitability, and to develop a complete set of pro-forma financial statements to indicate to prospective investors (a) how much money is required, (b) what will be done with the funds and (c) where will the company be in one, two and five years.

The Bank

One of the more important players in a turnaround is the company banker. His or her willingness or reticence to offer a generous and helping hand to the struggling company can become the deciding factor in the turnaround. If the bank manager believes in the turnaround strategy, and has confidence that the management can carry out the recovery plan, then the chances are that the line of credit will be established sufficiently high to permit the recovery.

In one of my failed attempts at a turnaround, the bank manager was so skeptical of the management abilities of the company share-holders that he allowed only collected receivables to be recycled into raw materials. Since collected receivables also had to pay for wages, salaries and other necessary overheads, the amount of money left over to purchase raw materials was insufficient to generate the volume of sales necessary to take the company out of its slump.

This situation is a guaranteed recipe for disaster, and I spent many heated phone calls trying to explain the situation to the bank manager. He insisted that he did not wish to "increase the bank's exposure," and the inevitable company failure ensued. I have always had difficulty understanding why the bank manager chose to close down the company and lose the bank's investment, rather than to risk a relatively small increase in exposure and save the company. But the example serves to indicate the fact that a lack of trust between the investor and the company management can make all the difference.

The Investors

There exists, even during difficult economic times, a large pool of available cash for investment. Taking into account all the wealthy families, the trust funds, the investment funds, the pension funds, and the turnaround and venture capital funds which exist with uncommitted cash at any given moment, it is safe to say that there are hundreds of millions of dollars available for investment. In times of recession, the owners and managers of these funds are more reticent to invest, but the money is there, seeking safe havens and secure investment, and occasionally it is there for high-risk ventures. The difficulty for the financially troubled company is not in locating the potential investors, but rather in convincing them to invest in the company.

In order to be convincing to prospective investors, any plans for the future should be bold and imaginative, but not unrealistic. It is difficult to describe in abstract terms how to be sufficiently bold but not overly optimistic. Real sales growth of 5% per annum may be considered quite normal and healthy for a financially stable company in a relatively mature industry, but certainly will not interest a prospective investor or institution who may be asked to risk hundreds of thousands if not millions of dollars. On the other hand, real sales growth of 30% per year in a company that has probably lost market share steadily for the past several years might strike even the most optimistic investor as "pie in the sky."

The person in charge of the turnaround must be able to sell the figures and the strategy to the investors in a quiet, convincing way, and this normally can only be done if the numbers reflect a well thought out and well conceived plan. Investors are not stupid people. They can, and usually do ask incisive, direct questions which are often very difficult to answer. It is not unusual after having tried to sell a plan to a particular investor or group of investors, that the turnaround person will have to re-think the recovery plan in light of the specific questions that were asked.

One cautionary note from personal experience: the private investors who are being approached may also have their own hidden agenda, which may not be consistent with the goals and objectives of the turnaround person. They may only want to find out as much as possible about the company, its financial weaknesses and its current plight, to enable them to plan a strategy for takeover to meet their own designs. These investors may try to negotiate secret deals with the major shareholders of the ailing company to take it over and force out certain members of management, or in some other way to de-rail ongoing efforts to effect an orderly recovery according to existing well laid plans. There are no rules that could be offered to warn the turnaround person of these pitfalls. Only experience and good judgement will prevail.

The Business Plan

The vision, the strategy and the recovery plan with its financial promises must be succinctly documented in a business plan. I have witnessed some very feeble attempts that pass for business plans. In one start-up case, I actually spent several weeks re-writing a business plan that had been put together by a playwright who had been interested in the project, and who had been retained to write the plan. The prose was exquisite, but I felt the plan lacked punch and clarity.

Besides the salesmanship of the turnaround person, the business plan is the only sales tool which enunciates the recovery plan of the company. It is this document which prospective investors take away with them for study, and upon which their entire decision-making process may be based. The business plan represents the only chance to persuade investors that yours is an excellent plan, and that of all the opportunities to invest at their disposal, yours is the one that is the most interesting, and holds the best promise for future gain.

The body of the report should be factual, simple, concise, succinct and to the point. Any detailed plans, lengthy descriptions or related incidental material which might detract from the central theme, or which could distract or side-track the reader, should be presented as an Appendix. Appendices can be as detailed and as long as necessary, and they leave the readers with the choice to read them or not to read them, at their discretion. Each heading should begin on a clean page, and there should be plenty of spacing between paragraphs.

The following is a typical outline for a business plan. It is worthwhile reviewing in brief detail some of the suggested techniques which will help to sell the plan.

Executive Summary

Keep the executive summary short and to the point, never more than two pages long. The purpose of the summary is to whet the apetite of the busy investor without forcing him to read more than he wishes, and to persuade him that it is worthwhile to read more detail in the body of the report.

History

Provide a brief historical note about the founding of the company, its growth, acquisitions, mergers, product line expansions and in general describe how the company came to be what it is.

Background

Describe what the company currently does, and include some information about its current size and product line. State briefly the reasons for the company's current difficulties, and the magnitude of the problems facing the company.

The Market

Write in some detail about the marketplace, the historical market growth, the future prospects and growth potential, the best merchandizing and marketing techniques for the company's product lines and any other relevant market details.

The Competition

Expose to the reader the strengths and weaknesses of the competitors, their pricing policies, warranty and customer service policies, and any other pertinent information that will advise the investor about the hurdles to be overcome in the marketplace.

The Recovery Plan

Describe in some detail the vision of where the company will be, and exactly how this vision will be achieved. Spend some time on the strategy to be used, and the market niche the company is going after. Describe the technical and structural advantages the company will possess.

The Management

Describe briefly the background, experience and strengths of each of the senior managers involved in the recovery effort.

Financial Opportunity

In this section, state clearly what the pro-forma financial statements indicate. Describe the sales growth, the cash flow improvement, shareholders' equity growth, anticipated profits, potential dividends, anticipated share value, return on new investment and any other indicators which would be of interest to a prospective investor.

A well written business plan can mean the difference between success and failure when soliciting investors.

 *Financing the Company*

Essentially, there are two basic ways to finance a company, and each of these two ways has several variations.

Equity Financing

If the turnaround plan has appeal, and the future of the company appears bright and worthy of risk-taking, then the most basic method of financing is equity financing. This means selling shares, or ownership in the company, and most investors who believe in a company's future will jump at the opportunity to become a part owner. The obvious motive for the equity investor is the potential for dividends and capital gain.

The problem for the existing owners is that most investors who are asked to place large sums at risk will demand a significant portion of the equity, sometimes amounting to control. This can be irksome to some owners. In extreme cases, owners would rather see their company fail than give away control to an outsider. Sometimes it is possible for owners to negotiate a buy-back deal with an investor, which would enable the owners to regain control of the troubled company once the turnaround becomes effective. Buy-back arrangements are not uncommon, but the investors will demand a significant return on their investment.

A typical medium- to high-risk investor may be looking for returns of between 35% and 50% per annum, and the person in charge of preparing the plans to revitalize the company must keep this fact in mind when preparing the turnaround scenario. The key question in the mind of the investor is, "What will my investment be worth in one year? In two years? In five years?" The answer to this question lies in the potential value of the shares, and there are several ways to evaluate share value.

One of the classic methods of evaluating the market value of a company is to take the estimated EBIT (earnings before interest and taxes) as calculated in the pro-forma financial statements, and apply a multiplier considered normal for that industry. Typical multipliers may range from very conservative values of 3 or 4 to more adventuresome values of 8 or higher, but a "quick and dirty" calculation using a multiplier of 5 will provide a reasonably conservative clue to potential market value of a going concern.

The real unknown, of course, is how many additional new shares might be issued at a future time. The requirement for additional financing down the road may cause significant share dilution, and the initial investors' equity position may have changed drastically. The original shareholders may find themselves left with a relatively small portion of a company which they once owned outright. These are the normal risks taken by equity investors.

Equity investments can be structured for voting shares or non-voting shares, and for participating or non-participating shares, and any combination thereof. For cautious investors who wish to hedge their risks it is possible to negotiate equity investment for preferred shares, and the higher the investment risk, the higher the dividend rate on the preferred shares. These preferred shares can be made convertible to common shares at some future time, as an inducement for the investor.

For the smaller company, there is also the possibility of approaching venture capital companies for equity funding. There are dozens of venture capital companies, and they vary in two essential ways. First, they vary in the amounts of financing they will provide. Some have minimum amounts of several million dollars, others have maximum amounts of several hundred thousand dollars. More importantly, they vary in their policies towards equity participation. Some venture lenders insist upon taking control, even up to 80% and more, while permitting the owners to buy back control over time, through earnings. Others do not want control, and will only insist upon a Board position to maintain a watchdog position over the company.

Debt Financing

Depending upon the debt-to-equity ratio of the company, it may also be possible to obtain additional debt financing. The advantage to this form of financing is that it does not affect the equity position of the shareholders, and the shares do not become diluted. The disadvantage is that the debt must be repaid periodically, without fail, along with interest. The interest rates offered to a financially troubled company considered to be a medium-to-high risk investment will not be favorable. Bank prime rate plus 2.5% or even higher is not uncommon.

All lending institutions will examine the amount of existing debt in the company, to determine whether the potential cash flow will be sufficient to repay the debt plus interest. A long-term-debt-to-equity ratio of 3:1 is considered to be approaching the maximum allowable. A total-debt-to-equity ratio (where "total debt" is the sum of long-term plus short-term debt) approaching 2:1 will light up a caution light to major lending institutions. In brief, the company's financial structure may simply not permit it to take on more long term debt than it already has, and this form of financing may not be an option.

Other Financing

There are, however, other avenues which may still be open to the ailing company. There exist companies whose business is to provide "mezzanine" financing to companies which are perceived to have an excellent chance for recovery and growth. Mezzanine financing is debt financing which is subordinated to the debt position of major lending institutions such as the chartered banks. Such lenders may demand slightly higher interest rates than the prime lenders, and will almost certainly want to take an equity position in the company, partly as a watchdog measure, and partly because of the potential for capital gain.

There are also various government-sponsored and labor union-sponsored funding agencies. For example, in Quebec the Societé de Développement Industriel du Québec (SDI), and the Fonds de Solidarité (FTQ union) are often willing to consider investing in Quebec-based companies which appear to have an excellent chance for recovery and growth. Such funding vehicles exist elsewhere, and it would be up to the person in charge of the turnaround to determine the availability of local financing agencies. Other provinces and the federal government have their own government sponsored lending institutions, as shown in Figure 15.

Figure 15: Selected Government Funding Agencies In Canada

FEDERAL
Federal Business Development Bank
Fednor (for Northern Ontario)
Western Diversification Program
Manufacturing Productivity Improvement Program (for Quebec)
Enterprise Development Program (for Quebec)
Atlantic Canada Opportunities Agency Action Program
Small Business Loans Act
BRITISH COLUMBIA
Small Business Venture Capital Program
ALBERTA
Alberta Opportunity Company
Alberta Research Council Joint Research Venture Program
SASKATCHEWAN
Saskatchewan Economic Development Corporation
ONTARIO
Innovation Ontario Corporation
Ontario Development Corporation
Northern Ontario Development Corporation
Eastern Ontario Development Corporation
The Northern Ontario Heritage Fund
QUEBEC
Quebec Industrial Development Corporation
NEW BRUNSWICK
Venture Capital Support Program
NOVA SCOTIA
Nova Scotia Business Capital Corporation
Nova Scotia Small Business Development Corporation
PRINCE EDWARD ISLAND
P.E.I. Development Agency
Prince Edward Island Lending Authority
NEWFOUNDLAND & LABRADOR
Newfoundland & Labrador Development Corporation

For the very small business with annual sales under $5 million, there are Federal government sponsored loans of up to $250 000. These loans are arranged by the chartered banks, whose duty it is to perform due diligence and to determine whether the asking business conforms to the fiscal requirements for a loan, and possesses a well-conceived recovery plan. Instead of the business being required to guarantee the loan, it is guaranteed by the Federal government, a fact that the lending banks find very comforting and reassuring when handing over the money.

Of course, all loans require collateral of some kind, and lending institutions will require some form of guarantee of repayment in case of default. In companies with private ownership, lending institutions will normally require signed personal guarantees from the owners, typically in the form of home or property mortgages signed over to the institution as collateral. This procedure can dissuade many an owner or group of owners from accepting institutional loans as a means of refinancing their ailing companies. This is especially true as owners become older, and become less willing to risk their family's financial future and security. Other forms of collateral would comprise the company's equipment, machinery and real estate, if these are available and have not already been pledged to lending institutions.

It is sometimes possible for a company to have its assets revalued upwards, if the accountants agree that this is feasible. This is a possibility, for example, where a machine shop realizes that it has a significant inventory of molds or special tooling on the floor which was never officially accounted for in the books. Such tooling can be worth hundreds of thousands of dollars, and can be capitalized. Or sometimes the machinery has been depreciated unduly quickly, and the company determines that the real market value far exceeds the depreciated value. In some cases, the auditing firm's accountants will permit the upward valuation of the machinery in question. Any upward revaluation of assets will provide increased collateral for additional loans, and can be a very useful tool.

Very often it is possible to negotiate favorable terms with lending institutions, in order to offer the best chance for a cash flow recovery. Government funding agencies will sometimes agree to waive interest repayment altogether for up to two years. Chartered banks will sometimes agree to capitalize the annual interest for a period of up to two years, so that a precarious cash flow is not overburdened during the recovery period. Principal repayments can also be postponed for a year or two. Debt investors can be quite flexible if they believe in the recovery plan.

One final word on collateral. Lending institutions are not in the business of looking after the homes, farms or the bankrupt assets of those owners whose companies have failed. In fact, large lending institutions do not always pursue those who are in default. In certain instances, institutions have been known to be less lenient with those whom they believe were dishonest or less than "up-front" in their dealings with the institution, and these people are sometimes pursued relentlessly by the institution. In other cases, the institutions have been known to settle for fifteen or twenty cents on the dollar, and are content not to further pursue the person in default.

Short-term Borrowing

There is a method sometimes used to modify the financial structure of an ailing company whose short term borrowing capacity has reached the maximum, and whose line of credit is extended to the limit. Short term debt can sometimes be converted into long term debt if the lending institution is in agreement. This move will permit a renewed line of credit, and will convert short term repayment schedules into long term repayments. Essentially, the company is exchanging current problems for future problems, with the expectation that the company will be better able to cope with repayment at a later time.

As a rule of thumb, the chartered banks will permit the short term loan or line of credit to reach a total of 75% of accounts receivable less than 90 days, plus 50% of the finished goods inventories. In some cases, work-in-process inventories may also be ascribed a value, stated as a percent of the selling price: around 35% would not be uncommon in a manufacturing industry. However, this is not always the case, and depending upon the performance of the company, and the perceived value of the inventories and receivables, these normal values can be modified upwards or downwards, at the bank's discretion. It is best for the turnaround person to inquire before making any assumptions that could affect the company's finances, with potentially disappointing results.

The person in charge of the turnaround should remember that at no time should a company borrow more than it needs to carry out a well-conceived and well-documented recovery plan. Borrowing is expensive in terms of its drain on the cash flow to service and repay the debt. Equity funding is also expensive in terms of the dividend payout requirements, and in some cases in terms of the penalty of lost equity and control.

There is another truism which a wise old Chief Financial Officer taught me many years ago, which has proved true over and over. Whenever investing money in a turnaround, always have as much again in your pocket to invest as the amount you first put in. The best laid recovery plans are bound to run aground on occasion, and more investment will almost surely be required before the recovery is a success. The person in charge of the turnaround should keep this fact in mind when seeking out investors.

The Last Resort

Sometimes, despite the efforts of the turnaround person and the management team, it becomes clear that the recovery plans simply are not going to work. Financing is not forthcoming. Equity investors are reticent to take the plunge, and the financial structure of the company will not permit further debt financing. The creditors are closing in, and are threatening to put the company into bankruptcy. Time is running short, and there appears to be no way out.

The "last resort," as it is meant to apply to this chapter, is for the ailing company to declare voluntary bankruptcy, and to prepare a proposal to its creditors before its creditors place the company into involuntary bankruptcy. The manoeuvre is risky at best. There are no guarantees that a proposal will be accepted, and the mere act of declaring voluntary bankruptcy may signal the end of operations. The move is not to be taken lightly. It is truly a last resort, to be considered only when the shareholders and the Board of Directors feel that there is no reasonable alternative.

Angry creditors can be an unpredictable lot. Obviously, no-one likes to wait indefinitely to receive monies owed, and the reactions of creditors differ widely to this circumstance. Some will complain bitterly over only a few hundred dollars, and will threaten to take legal action. Often they will become abusive over the telephone, and will shout obscenities at the hapless accounts payable clerk, who is powerless to remedy the situation. Others will ask politely for a demonstration of good faith, and will request that the offending company simply send a cheque for a token amount of one or two hundred dollars to indicate their willingness to keep the relationship alive. All too often, however, even this token gesture is impossible for the cash-starved company.

In some cases, particularly obstinate suppliers will refuse to continue to do business with the delinquent company even on a COD basis. This reaction has always surprised me, because it seems to me that if the ailing company can be helped to overcome its difficulties by an understanding and sympathetic supplier, the recovering company will, in turn, remain an extremely grateful and loyal customer. The lost monies would be repaid many times over in the long run. Obviously, not all suppliers view the world in the same way.

Very often, in order to maintain good accounting practices, creditors will insist that the delinquent company pay its debts even if there is an offsetting receivable from the same creditor. "You send me a cheque for what you owe me, and then I'll send you a cheque for what I owe you." How simple life would be if one could convince the creditor to simply offset one invoice against the other, leaving only the difference to worry about. However, strict adherence to procedure can override common sense.

Both the United States and Canada have provisions in their laws which permit an ailing company to file for temporary protection from its creditors, aimed at providing the company an opportunity to develop a plan which will nurture it back to health. In Canadian statutes there is Chapter C-36, which provides the opportunity for a stricken company to negotiate terms with its creditors. In the United States, Chapter 11 of the Bankruptcy Act provides this opportunity. Both cases involve a declaration of voluntary bankruptcy, and a proposal to creditors.

Although both countries provide the legal means for companies to avail themselves of temporary protection from their creditors, the procedures are not identical. The United States is generally more "entrepreneur-friendly" than is Canada, and this trend is evident when comparing "Chapter 11" to "Chapter C-36." The Canadian procedure is rigorous, and success is by no means assured. The American procedure is less strict, although success can be equally elusive.

The Canadian Procedure

The first step for the ailing Canadian company to take is to locate a friendly trustee to act on its behalf. The word "friendly" is used to underscore the fact that the trustee must be dedicated to helping the company's cause, and must not be actively involved in conflicting mandates. The choice of trustees is critical. The trustee used by the company's lending bank, for example, would not be an unbiased trustee. An experienced trustee will be of invaluable assistance, and will not only be completely familiar with all aspects of the Bankruptcy Act, but also will advise the ailing company on matters of procedure, how much to offer creditors, and what payment schedules are most likely to be accepted. The fees charged by trustees are not insignificant, and payment of such fees must be carefully negotiated and clearly understood.

Once the decision is made to hire a trustee and to prepare a proposal to creditors, and the trustee has been so informed in writing, the trustee then has five days to notify all the creditors of the intent to make a proposal. This notification prevents any further legal action from being taken by creditors against the company. The first task of the trustee is to carefully gather all information about the accounts payable and the accounts receivable, to verify the accuracy of each account, and then to divide the information into secured and unsecured creditors. Not surprisingly, governments are highest on the pecking order, and all unpaid deductions at source (DAS) and back-taxes are first on the list. It is worthy of note that in Canada today, directors of companies are jointly and severally liable for unpaid DAS. Next come the institutional lenders such as the chartered banks. These, too, are usually secured creditors right behind the governments.

Employees, consultants, shareholders and suppliers are unsecured creditors, and are lumped into this category by the trustee in descending order of the amount owed to each creditor. It becomes important that amounts owing are clearly understood, agreed to and nailed down.

Within ten days after the official hiring of the trustee, the lists of monies owed to both secured and unsecured creditors must be completed, and a detailed statement must be sent to each creditor who requests it, showing the expected revenues and outflows which can be reasonably expected by the company, including the list of creditors and how much each is owed. The trustee has 30 days from the date of his official hiring to discuss with the shareholders and/or the Board of Directors the details of the proposal, specifically what amount to offer, and when to pay it. This official proposal must be filed with the government.

After officially filing the proposal, the trustee must send a copy of the proposal to the creditors, along with a current balance sheet of the company. The trustee has a maximum of 21 days to set up and hold a meeting with the creditors to try to obtain acceptance of the proposal. Although these time limits and constraints may seem confusing and restrictive, they are legal requirements and must be adhered to without deviation.

Once the creditors know there is going to be a proposal, and once they know the details of the amount offered and the repayment schedule, it is important for a senior manager of the debtor company to contact each creditor and try to convince him to accept the terms of the proposal. This is true for both the secured and the unsecured creditors. Contacting each and every creditor is time-consuming, and at times discouraging.

In order for a proposal to creditors to be accepted, the rule is that a majority in number (50% plus one) and two-thirds in value (66.67% of the dollars owed) must agree to the proposal. Since these parameters apply to the total numbers and not just to those who voted, it becomes doubly important to persuade as many creditors as possible to vote in favor of the proposal. In a proposal to creditors, only the votes of the unsecured creditors count toward the ultimate decision to accept or reject the proposal.

If the secured creditors also agree by a majority in number and two thirds of the value, then they too will be bound by the decision. If, however, the secured creditors do not agree within these margins, then they are not bound by the outcome of the vote, and they may proceed to take action under the provisions of the Bankruptcy Act.

If the vote is negative and the proposal is rejected, the debtor company has 45 days to make a new proposal, if it wishes to do so, and if the courts grant the permission. In all, there can be several extensions as long as these extensions do not exceed five months in total. If, as and when a proposal is accepted, the debtor company is protected from all unsecured creditors, including landlords and leasing agents, and has the right to continue to use its assets, even those secured by the lending institutions, in the course of pursuing its normal daily business.

The repayment plan as agreed to by the creditors must, of course, be adhered to rigidly. If, for example, the proposal agreed to repay the first 5 cents on the dollar after twelve months, then this agreement must be respected to the letter. If the debtor company is in default due to a lower than expected cash flow, then the game is over, and the company is considered in bankruptcy.

The American Procedure

The first step for the ailing American company is to file a petition with the clerk of the bankruptcy court for protection under Chapter 11, which automatically becomes an order for relief. The action of filing for relief protects the debtor from pursuit by creditors for all debts incurred up to the moment of filing. Within 20 days of receipt of the order for relief, the company must send notice of the voluntary bankruptcy filing to all creditors as well as to the Securities Exchange Commission, the Internal Revenue Service and the local United States Attorney. The company has 30 days to file a complete list of its creditors, both secured and unsecured, and a list of equity security holders. It must also file a set of up-to-date financial statements and a complete list of assets.

Generally speaking, there is no necessity for the ailing company to obtain a trustee. Under normal circumstances the head of the company is automatically considered a "debtor in possession," and is given all the powers of a trustee to continue to operate the company, complete with compensation. Only if the creditors suspect irregularities or fraudulent activities, or if they have reason to doubt the company's ability or its willingness to come up with a practical workout plan, or if there is some question as to the management's competence, would the creditors request the courts to appoint a trustee. Such appointment could be made at any time.

The creditors have 25 days within which to file objections, after receiving their notice from the company of its intent to file for bankruptcy under Chapter 11. The company must convene a meeting with the creditors between 20 and 40 days after receiving the order for relief. Meanwhile, as soon as practical, the court will appoint at least one Committee of Creditors to ensure that the company is proceeding in accordance with agreed plans. The usual make-up of this committee comprises the seven largest unsecured claim holders who are willing to serve on the committee. There can also be a committee appointed comprising the seven largest equity interest holders. Where applicable, the court can also appoint a committee which consists of retired employees actively receiving benefits.

If the company is unionized, the debtor in possession has the right to submit a reasonable proposal to the employees' union to modify the work rules, wage structure and benefits package, to help the company work its way out of financial difficulty. The court will act as final arbiter, but the union cannot reject a reasonable workout proposal without good cause. It must be said that under no circumstances should Chapter 11 be used simply as a vehicle to wriggle out of a difficult labor contract, and if it is perceived that this is happening, the courts will not find favorably toward the debtor in possession.

From the time the company receives the order for relief, it has 120 days to develop and submit a workout plan to work its way out of difficulty. This time period can be modified by the courts. The creditor committees can assist in the formulation of the workout plan. The plan can include hiring new officers, disposal of assets, extension of scheduled payments, a reduction of payments to its creditors, mergers, amendments to the company charter, issuing securities and equity, and any other plans considered legal. The plan must be acceptable to all parties, and treat all classes of creditor fairly. The debtor in possession must furnish the creditors with sufficient information so that they can make an informed decision whether to accept or reject the plan. It should be noted that any of the creditors can also file a workout plan, and it is up to the courts to decide which of the plans submitted is the fairest and best.

The stricken company has 60 days after filing its workout plan in which to obtain creditor acceptance. In the case of secured and unsecured creditors, acceptance requires 50% plus one in number of creditors and two-thirds of the dollar amount. For equity interest holders, acceptance requires two-thirds of the dollar amount. It is important to remember that in all cases these parameters apply only to the number of actual votes cast, and not to the total number of creditors.

The court then will provide 25 days' notice for a hearing on the confirmation of the workout plan. Any class of creditor being offered 100 cents on the dollar will be deemed by the court to have accepted the plan, and any class of creditor offered zero cents on the dollar will be deemed to have refused the plan. If all classes of creditors accept the plan as submitted, then the courts will confirm the plan as final. The plan can be modified and reworked as often as necessary prior to the time of confirmation, and creditors must file any objections prior to confirmation. The creditors can vote again each time there is a modification.

The court will confirm the workout plan if all the classes of creditors have accepted it. However, the court will confirm a workout plan even if one class of creditor has rejected it, provided the plan is considered by the court to be fair and equitable to all classes of creditor. The court will even confirm the plan if the dissenting class of creditor is secured, provided the court is reasonably convinced that the secured creditors will receive the equivalent of their claims in property. This is known as a "cram down" provision, and it is important to remember that this provision will not be instituted by the court unless it has been specifically requested by the debtor in possession.

The court can refuse confirmation of the plan if there is judged to be good cause, and the court reserves the right at any time to dismiss the case, or force liquidation of the assets. Once confirmed, there is no time limit other than the plan's own timetable for the plan to work itself out, but the court will insist that all taxes owing shall be paid within 120 days after confirmation.

Pitfalls

Governments do not capitulate easily. They tend to present a stony exterior, and will not readily accept anything less than 100 cents on the dollar. Certainly this is true with respect to past-due deductions at source and back taxes. They can become more lenient with respect to the repayment of loans, but the effort required to convince governments to buy into a proposal is great. One of the problems when dealing with governments is that one must deal with a huge bureaucracy, and the person to whom you are relegated on the telephone will be a minor civil servant who is programmed to give only one reply. This person is certainly not prepared to make a firm decision, and the case is invariably referred to their supervisor, who is almost always impossible to reach. Unlike companies, governments tend to make decisions at the highest possible level, and decision-makers are rare.

Dealing with the banks or lending institutions may be easier, but not necessarily more successful. The loan manager may not wish to be accomodating, if he feels that the debtor company was not entirely up-front in its dealings with the institution. Whether the loan manager wants to go along with the proposal is a judgement call, but even if it is decided to go along with the proposal, the higher management of the lending institution may overrule that decision. Banks are by nature low-risk lenders, and they are averse to high risk situations. On the brighter side, one loan manager with whom I dealt in a proposal to creditors stated that banks look upon the reduction of debt as being equivalent to the creation of equity. In general, however, secured creditors hold the majority of the cards, and it is best to assume that their debts will probably have to be paid, if not in full, then certainly in large measure.

Dealing with the unsecured creditors can also be an adventure in frustration. In one case, I spoke to the chief accountant of a well-known multinational corporation to whom we owed a large amount of money. I was immediately referred to their legal department. Their attorneys told me in no uncertain terms that our proposal would be refused. The amount we owed this particular creditor far outweighed all the others, so it was extremely important that I get them to approve our proposal. I pleaded with them, telling them that we would enable them to recover much of their loss through years of future business, but to no avail. They steadfastly refused my request. And yet, on voting day, the corporation accepted our proposal meekly, as if nothing had happened.

Some small creditors snarled their defiance, threatening to go as far as the law would permit in their pursuit of us, and in fact were true to their word on voting day. They voted against the proposal. There is simply no way to be sure in advance how creditors will vote. The previous relationship with the debtor company seems to play an important role in the final outcome.

I was involved in a case where there was an argument between the shareholders and an employee about exactly how much was owed the employee. A promise had been made to the employee in writing that he would be given shares instead of cash in return for services rendered. The letter had never been signed by the shareholders, and the promise had not been kept. The internal squabbling was vicious, and certainly did not help the trustee, who had to deal with all parties and bring the argument to a negotiated conclusion. It seems that proposals to creditors are never simple matters, and can be fraught with problems that appear out of the woodwork.

To anyone who hasn't lived through a proposal to creditors, the process may seem nerve-wracking. A typical offering to creditors might be in the vicinity of 20 to 35 cents on the dollar, and to the first-time participant such a low offering may seem doomed to certain failure. Furthermore, a typical repayment schedule may take one year or more, and may involve a series of minute payments, which to the first-time participant may appear certain to be unacceptable to the creditors. It is adviseable to seek the advice of an expert who has had considerable experience in these matters and who will be able to judge what will pass as acceptable.

The Fallout

There are myriad rules which govern the bankruptcy laws, and in particular the process of a proposal to creditors. Furthermore, the laws are constantly being amended. It is not the intention of this book to cover the law in detail, but rather to advise the turnaround person that this alternative does exist, albeit fraught with peril and uncertainty. Voluntary bankruptcy tends to cause a loss of public confidence in the company, and weakens the relationship with creditors. The confidence of banks and other lending institutions becomes undermined.

The proposal to creditors is truly a last resort, to be seriously considered only after all other avenues have been exhausted.

A Final Word

The task of turning around whole companies, or even divisions or just departments, is certainly not for everyone. It is an exhausting and time consuming task, sometimes thankless, often filled with frustrations, and certainly not always successful. It should not be undertaken by sensitive souls, who will agonize over the unpleasant decisions which must inevitably be taken.

On the other hand, the exhilaration and satisfaction that can be derived from successfully turning a sick company around, and saving the jobs of employees, some of whom didn't even believe the company was in serious trouble, is worth the effort for some people. I am one of those people, and I have thoroughly enjoyed my years in the turnaround field.

Appendix I

Critical Questions for Systematic Company Analysis and Diagnosis

Administration

– What is the corporate culture, and is it desireable?
– Is the reporting structure clear?
– Is the company structured for effective delegation and control?
– Do the key managers appear competent and knowledgeable in their field?
– Are there clear job descriptions for the senior management positions?
– Can management, technical and clerical staff be reduced, or positions combined, without materially affecting the ability of the company to function?
– Is Sales, Production and Financial data and information gathering accurate, complete and pertinent?
– Is information distributed to the right people, in timely fashion to permit fast action or reaction?
– Are reports easily understood, and are the formats efficient?
– Does senior management have a clear vision of the objectives of the company, and the strategy to achieve these objectives?
– Does the accounting department have a good grasp of the cost items, and does it closely monitor variances from the budget?

Finance

– Are there Balance Sheet comparisons for the past five years for at least the following key parameters:
  * Current ratio (working capital availability)
  * Quick ratio (indication of liquidity)
  * A/R and A/P days (indication of cash management ability)
  * Long term debt and total debt to equity ratios (borrowing position)
  * Retained earnings position (attractiveness to investors)
  * Inventory turnovers (indication of excess inventories)

- Are there Profit and Loss Statement comparisons for the past five years for at least the following key parameters:
  * Material and labor costs as a percentage of sales (direct cost control)
  * Gross margin percent (health of the operations)
  * Selling, Administrative and Financial expenses as a percent of Sales (indication of cost control)
  * Individual line items as a percent of Sales (indication of cost control)
  * The Return on Sales and on Invested Assets (attractiveness to investors)
  * The Earnings Before Interest and Taxes (EBIT) (indication of company value)
- Are there detailed monthly Operating, Selling and Capital Expenditure budgets?
- Are there weekly or monthly Cash Flow projections?
- What has been the past three years' capital investment compared to prior years?
- What immediate capital investment is required to regain productivity levels for competitive advantage?
- What is the next three years' long term debt repayment schedule?
- How realistic is the work-in-process and finished goods inventory evaluation?
- Are product costs known and tracked?
- Is sufficient effort being exerted on credit analysis and cash collection?
- Are there any projects which could be cut or postponed without hurting the immediate functioning of the company?
- Is there any office, factory, rolling stock or productive equipment which could be sold outright for cash, or sold for leaseback to yield cash?
- Does the company own any land or buildings which could be sold, rented or sold for leaseback to yield cash?
- Is there future cash recovery potential through Research and Development credits?

- Have all management, technical and clerical staff bonuses, salary increases (promised or otherwise) and shareholder dividend payments been cancelled?
- Would closing part of the operations or discontinuing a product line improve profitability?
- Have tight control measures been put in place to monitor "loose" expenditure items such as Travel, Entertainment, Long distance phone, Office supplies and Small tools?
- Are the owners milking the company?
    * Verify dividend history
    * Verify fees paid to owners
    * Verify expense accounts and automobiles
    * Verify uncollected A/R from owners' other companies
- What magnitude of capital infusion is required to effect a proper turnaround and provide needed working capital?
    * Does the current capital structure allow for more long-term debt?
    * Would the current owners accept a dilution of equity?
    * Is a capital restructuring of the company advised?
    * Are government aid programs available and applicable?
- Have Pro-Forma financial statements been prepared to show what the turnaround plan might achieve?

Industrial Relations
- Is the union militant, and what is the company's strike history?
- When does the current union contract expire, and what are the expected demands in the next negotiations?
- How many grievances are currently outstanding?
- Is the union likely to agree to a wage freeze or wage cut?
- What percentage of grievances are normally settled at the supervisory level?
- Are the supervisors competent leaders and communicators?
- Are there clear job descriptions for hourly and clerical positions?

- How do the wage and salary levels fit into the industry scales?
- What are the fringe benefits as a percent of wages?
- Is there an incentive plan, and how much does it pay out?
- What is the next scheduled wage increase in the union contract?
- How have clerical and supervisors' salaries kept up with union wage increases over the years?

Manufacturing

- What are the gross sales per employee?
- Does the company habitually lay off personnel as the sales activity drops off?
- Are there useful measurements of productivity in terms of output per employee hour?
- Does the workforce appear reasonably occupied?
- What is the accident and safety record?
- Does the purchasing function appear knowledgeable and competent?
- Is there a competent production scheduling and production expediting function?
- What is the level of late deliveries of orders?
- What is the record of critical inventory stock-outs?
- Are scrap and rework quantities measured?
- How much of the raw materials and finished goods inventories are slow moving?
- Is there a pilferage or shrinkage problem?
- Is there an accredited quality assurance program?
- What is the rate of quality and warranty returns as a percent of sales?
- What is the level of overtime premiums as a percent of labor cost?
- What is the ratio of direct to indirect labor?
- Is there an effective preventive maintenance system in use?

- What is the equipment downtime rate for breakdowns, preventive maintenance, lack of spare parts, out of raw materials, out of orders?
- What is maintenance cost as a percentage of original equipment cost?
- How modern is the equipment, and what portion remains undepreciated?
- What is the degree of difficulty of the technology, and what is the probability of replacing specialists and technicians on short notice?

Sales And Marketing

- How much damage has the company name suffered in the marketplace?
- Are there realistic sales projections by product, by salesperson, by territory?
- Is the company's market share known?
- Is the competition and its strengths and weaknesses well understood?
- Are competitive pricing policies known?
- Does the estimating procedure and the pricing policy make sense?
- Are individual product costs known and tracked, and are the product lines profitable?
- Are requests for quotations handled quickly and efficiently?
- Does the purchasing function have sufficient alternative suppliers to maintain cost advantages?
- Is the targeted market well understood?
- Does the advertising program and promotional literature campaign make economic sense?
- Are salespersons assigned to products or territories effectively?
- Is there a working customer service function in place?
- What is the cost of the quality and product warranty program as a percentage of sales?
- What is the level of price discounts as a percentage of sales?

- Does the sales force and/or the distributor network contain weak links?
- Can sales commissions be reduced or renegotiated?
- Does the merchandising and distribution strategy make sense?
- Are there realistic plans to increase market share?
- Is there a coherent plan for product development or new product introduction?

Appendix II

Sample Listings of Senior Managers' Job Duties

A Sample Listing of a President's Duties

Position: President

Reports To: Board of Directors

Position Description: To ensure that the company is operated on a profitable basis; that it is properly financed, equipped and staffed; and to carry out the necessary strategic planning to ensure the future growth and survival of the company.

Typical Responsibility: The production manager, the marketing manager, the finance manager, the personnel manager, the research & development manager and one executive secretary.

List Of Duties:
1. To ensure that the senior management team is competent, and that the team functions as a cohesive unit.
2. To ensure that the middle management structure is lean and effective, and operates in a co-operative team effort.
3. To ensure that the labor force is properly trained and motivated to perform to required output and quality standards.
4. To ensure the implementation of proper safety and environmental standards.
5. To ensure that all labor agreements conform to industry standards, and that they do not restrict the operations of the company by reducing its competitiveness.
6. To ensure that the salary and wage structures are competitive within industry standards.
7. To provide appropriate motivating bonus and performance plans to key personnel or positions.

8. To ensure that the capital equipment is properly maintained and that it is capable of the output levels required to maintain the company in a competitive position.

9. To approve the annual operating and capital expenditure budgets.

10. To approve the marketing, sales and advertising budgets.

11. To ensure that the marketing, merchandising and distribution methods of the company are the best to achieve maximum sales and market penetration.

12. To ensure the profitability of the product lines and the company through appropriate accounting practices and financial reporting.

13. To ensure that the company is properly financed, and that the financial structure is sound.

14. To develop contacts with financial institutions.

15. To determine the advances in industry technology, and to decide what steps must be taken to advance the technical level of the company.

16. To determine the extent of product development and research activities for the company.

17. To locate potential strategic alliance partners and technical alliance partners locally and abroad.

18. To determine the future direction of the company in terms of growth through increased sales and market penetration, through expansion into foreign markets, through addition of product lines, or through acquisition strategy.

19. To negotiate sales and technical alliances as required to carry out the corporate growth objectives.

20. To identify potential acquisition targets.

21. To oversee all news and press releases concerning company activities.

22. Be aware of the constant threat of potential market domination and/or takeover by key competitors.

A Sample Listing of a Manufacturing Director's Duties

Position: Manufacturing Director

Reports To: President

Position Description: To effectively manage the manpower, machines and materials in the areas of manufacturing, to achieve the objectives of the company.

Typical Responsibility: Four production supervisors; one maintenance supervisor, one Quality Control technician; one production scheduler, one production expediter.

List Of Duties:

1. To manage the department within the constraints of the Operating Budgets, and to ship out the product in accordance with the sales department requirements.
2. To ensure that sufficient qualified and trained workers are on site as required to accomplish the scheduled workload, and to react quickly to lay-off excess personnel as and when the workload diminishes.
3. To ensure that at least minimum safety standards are followed, and that there are sufficient first aid kits, fire extinguishers and stretchers installed and in good working order, as well as sufficient heating and ventilation.
4. To be familiar with and to follow the requirements of government regulations.
5. To ensure that all machinery, equipment and rolling stock is well maintained and in safe and proper working order.
6. To ensure that cleanliness and housekeeping in the shop, warehouses, truck bay, washrooms, lunch room and offices is maintained to a good and decent standard.

7. To ensure that all employee time cards are kept up to date and properly verified.

8. To provide all required production and distribution reports and paperwork, correctly filled out and completed on time.

9. To supervise the daily activities of the department supervisors, the QC technician and the expediter.

10. To oversee the management of the scheduling, the workload and needs of the employees, and to properly interpret and apply the collective agreement.

11. To oversee the quality control funtion, and to follow the Quality Assurance manual directives, such that the department will maintain its QA accreditation at all times.

12. To ensure that all QC testing equipment is in proper working order.

13. To ensure that all QC testing equipment is properly calibrated and periodically verified.

14. To ensure that all QC test procedures are properly carried out in accordance with the QA manual.

15. To ensure that all QC test results and paperwork is properly filed for product traceability and test verification, and that files are properly maintained for the legal time limits.

16. To work in close collaboration with the sales department to achieve on-time delivery of all merchandise.

17. To work in close collaboration with the Customer Service group, to ensure that rush or emergency shipments are made to satisfy customers' needs.

18. To work in collaboration with the materials and supplies buyer, to ensure adequate stocks of raw materials and supplies to complete the orders on hand.

19. To be continually aware of the order status and the order backlog for the department, and to work closely with the buyer to eliminate the backlog as quickly as possible.

20. To operate and schedule the department to ensure the least waste of material, time and energy, and that the

lowest number of personnel is maintained to adequately perform the required work.

21. To ensure on-time delivery of the merchandise or finished product, in accordance with the customers' demands.

22. To ensure that the customer receives the correct material in the correct quantities, as ordered by the customer.

23. To ensure that all returned merchandise and defective merchandise is handled in accordance with the procedures outlined in the QA manual.

24. To ensure that all incoming materials counts and checks are performed in accordance with the QA manual, and that certificates of compliance are issued as required.

25. To ensure that the physical inventories are accurately and efficiently taken as required or as requested.

26. To provide adequate and efficient storage areas and racking for both raw materials and finished product, optimizing the use of available space.

27. To provide technical assistance to customers when called upon to do so.

28. To assist the sales department with quotations by providing the necessary technical information and specifications as requested.

29. To ensure the timely preparation of the annual operating budgets in accordance with company policy and constraints.

30. To ensure the timely preparation of the annual capital expenditure budgets for the manufacturing departments, in accordance with company policy and constraints.

31. To report to superiors all problem areas which might impede the proper carrying out of assigned duties.

32. All other tasks and assignments as may be requested by superiors.

A Sample Listing of a Marketing Director's Duties

Position: Marketing Director

Reports To: President

Position Description: To develop marketing strategies and to oversee the activities of sales personnel to achieve the objectives of the company.

Typical Responsibility: four outside salespersons, two inside salespersons, one customer service rep, one secretary; one sales agent, two distributors.

List Of Duties:
1. To achieve the sales levels as outlined in the sales projections.
2. To determine policy with respect to sales territories, and coverage by salespersons, agents and/or distributors.
3. To determine merchandising and distribution policies, with respect to the use of sales outlets, agents and distributors.
4. To prepare coherent strategies to increase market penetration.
5. To determine finished goods inventory policies with respect to consignment at customers' premises.
6. To prepare sales targets and objectives, by product, by territory and by sales person or outlet.
7. To prepare sales projections by period, by year.
8. To establish discount schedules and policies.
9. To establish pricing policies and estimating procedures.
10. To prepare warranty and quality returns policies.
11. To prepare the annual sales and marketing budgets in accordance with company policies and constraints.

12. To prepare the advertising plans and budgets, and to oversee the preparation of copy for brochures, pamphlets, media advertising and magazine ads.

13. To ensure that sufficient information is known about competitors, their strengths and weaknesses, and their pricing policies.

14. To be responsible for the Customer Service function, and to ensure that service levels are consistent with company policies.

15. To be responsible for the New Product Development function, and to add new products and new product lines which will maintain or improve the company's gross margins, and will substantially increase the company's sales levels, in accordance with the company policies.

16. To directly manage the salespersons, both those outside on the road, and those inside at the order desk, and to ensure that their activities are productive and directed toward achieving the company's sales goals.

17. To hire and train new salespersons, as required, both outside on the road and inside at the order desk, and to continue the development of existing salespersons, as required in order to achieve sales targets.

18. To operate within the constraints of the established sales and marketing expense budgets.

19. To develop and maintain an excellent relationship with all customers, with special emphasis on large important accounts, both through telephone contact and through personal visits.

20. To open up targeted new accounts, and to help develop new territories, through periodic field trips.

21. To be responsible for the preparation of timely and accurate estimates, and to follow-up on all quotations.

22. To ensure the fair distribution of accounts to all outside salespersons, and to oversee house accounts.

23. To negotiate fair commission rates and fee structures for company sales personnel, as well as sales agents and distributors.

24. To ensure that the customer's technical requirements are properly answered.

25. To oversee the company advertising budgets, and to ensure that advertising copy is prepared and placed in the appropriate publications and other media in timely manner.

26. To determine inasmuch as possible the tangible return on the company's advertising dollars.

27. To ensure that appropriate copy is prepared for brochures and promotional literature, and that a sufficient supply of promotional documentation is on hand and distributed at all times.

28. To maintain a close liaison with the manufacturing manager to ensure that sufficient resources are on hand to meet customers' technical and delivery demands.

29. To work closely with the production personnel to ensure that delivery and quality requirements are properly met.

30. To perform all other functions and tasks as may be required by superiors from time to time.

A Sample Listing of a Financial Director's Duties

Position: Finance Director

Reports To: President

Position Description: To ensure that proper accounting practices and procedures are followed, that the company assets are properly accounted for, that adequate financing is in place, and that all covenants and administrative policies are adhered to.

Typical Responsibility: One bookkeeper, one accounts-receivable clerk, one accounts-payable clerk, one credit & collections clerk, one receptionist and one general secretary.

List Of Duties:

1. Ensure that an appropriate code of accounts is maintained and properly adhered to by the accounting staff, and that the various cost elements are posted to the proper accounts.
2. Ensure that accurate accounts receivable ledgers and aging lists are maintained and updated regularly.
3. Ensure that accounts receivable are collected in timely fashion, and that appropriate action is taken to rectify delinquent accounts.
4. Ensure that appropriate credit limits are imposed on new accounts, and that credit limits on existing accounts are continuously updated.
5. Ensure that the cash receipts are posted regularly and kept up-to-date.
6. Ensure that the bank reconciliations are properly carried out.
7. Ensure that accurate accounts payable ledgers and aging lists are maintained and updated regularly.

8. Ensure that materials receipts are matched with appropriate receiving slips and verified for cost and quantity received.
9. Ensure that a secure system of issuing cheques is in place to prevent double payment of invoices, and to prevent unauthorized cheques from being issued.
10. Ensure that period-end closings are performed properly and in keeping with accepted accounting principles, and that all financial reports are issued in timely fashion.
11. Oversee all general ledger postings and adjustments, and assist where necessary to ensure that the trial balance is correct, and that the balance sheets represent fairly and accurately the company financial position.
12. Ensure that periodic inventory counts are quickly and accurately taken, and costed in accordance with company policies.
13. Ensure that all necessary schedules are properly prepared in advance for year-end audit, minimize the auditors' task.
14. Manage the working capital of the company by paying close attention to inventory levels, accounts payable levels and accounts receivable.
15. Manage the company's bank accounts, and ensure that the appropriate cash transfers are made to cover the expenditures.
16. Ensure that periodic cash flow projections are performed and followed-up to predict potential cash flow problems.
17. Closely scrutinize the period-end financial reports, and prepare reasons and explanations for significant variances from normal or budgeted figures.
18. Ensure the preparation of the annual operating budgets in accordance with company policies with the input of the department managers.
19. Ensure the preparation of the annual capital expenditure budgets in accordance with company policies with the input of the department managers.

20. Ensure that an appropriate product costing system is in place and that the profitability of each product and product line is adequately monitored.

21. Ensure that adequate fire, theft and business interruption insurance is maintained for the company's assets; that adequate key employee insurance is maintained; and that adequate indemnity and product liability insurance is maintained.

22. Maintain accurate records of fixed asset inventories, together with appropriate cost and depreciation records.

23. Maintain continual contact with the bank manager or account manager to provide accurate accounting information as requested by the lending institution.

24. Negotiate loans and interest payments as required to provide sufficient operating capital to satisfy the company's needs, within the established operating covenants.

25. Oversee on a continuous basis the various critical operating and financial ratios to ensure the continuous financial health of the company.

26. To oversee the staff and clerical positions, and to ensure that properly trained personnel is available to fill these positions as required.

27. To act as an advisor to the various department managers who may be having difficulty preparing budgets, interpreting financial data or operating within the given budget constraints as imposed by the company.

28. Ensure that all company forms and reports are up-to-date, accurate and circulated in timely fashion to those who require the information to carry out their functions.

29. Oversee the company office and computer supply stores.

30. Determine the purchasing policies of the company, and to oversee the requisitioning practices.

31. Ensure that records-keeping and the company archives are maintained to required standards.

32. Ensure that all necessary government and institutional paperwork is completed, including taxation, payroll and insurance forms.

33. Negotiate all leases for buildings, equipment and rolling stock, and oversee all property rental agreements.

34. Form part of the union negotiating team, and ensure that all union demands are accurately costed for potential impact on company finances and future competitiveness.

35. Perform such other tasks, duties and special assignments as may be assigned by superiors.

A Sample Listing of a Human Resources Director's Duties

Position: Human Resources Director

Reports To: President

Position Description: To ensure the availability of a trained, motivated and competent management, technical and clerical staff and labor-force; to manage the labor contracts and to ensure a good working relationship between the company and the labor-force.

Typical Responsibility: One human relations specialist, one human resources clerk and one secretary.

List Of Duties:

1. To search for personnel to fill vacant positions in the managerial, technical and clerical staff, as well as the labor-force.
2. To establish entry criteria for all positions.
3. To perform the interviewing and screening of all candidates for positions at all levels.
4. To hold exit interviews with all personnel leaving the company.
5. To establish the rules of employee conduct on company premises, and to determine and apply disciplinary action for non-compliance.
6. To establish job evaluation procedures, and to ensure that wage scales follow job evaluation guidelines.
7. To establish the managerial, technical and clerical position salary scales.
8. To establish and apply the bonus and/or incentive schemes in accordance with company policy.

9. To establish appropriate fringe benefits packages for the various employee categories, in accordance with company policy.

10. To assist the various department heads in the day-to-day interpretation and application of the labor agreements.

11. To follow-up on all grievances, and to assist the department heads with appropriate responses to grievances.

12. To act as the final company authority in the interpretation and handling of labor disputes.

13. To act as the chief negotiator for the company during all labor contract negotiations.

14. To maintain up-to-date labor contracts of competitors and related industries.

15. To alert the president of the implications of all union demands.

16. To handle and act upon employee complaints, disputes and discontent.

17. To take appropriate action in the event of the death or marriage of employees and their close relatives, or in the event of the birth of children to employees.

18. To fill out records and forms as required by various governments or agencies, such as unemployment forms and medical forms.

19. To maintain complete employee records for the company.

20. To complete all other tasks and projects as requested by superiors.

Appendix III

The Elements of a Quality Assurance Program

Preamble

A properly functioning Quality Assurance (QA) program will assist the company in the following ways:

1. It will instill an awareness of quality at all levels of the company, thereby reducing the production of waste product, scrap and sub-standard product;

2. It will permit the company to bid on jobs not accessible to companies which do not possess structured QA programs;

3. It will permit the company to continue to do its existing business with those customers who have made compliance with a formal QA program a necessity.

The tangible benefits which can be expected from the installation of a structured QA program are:

1. Reduced operating costs.

2. Increased market share.

3. Increased export market potential.

It is important that (a) the willingness to live with, and (b) the willingness to follow rigorously the demands of a formal QA program must come from top management. If the senior management is not committed to the QA program, then the program will fail.

It should be clearly understood by top management that the greater the complexity of the quality control system, the greater the benefits. However, the more complex the system becomes, the more expensive it is to maintain, and the higher the overhead costs.

The QA Function within the Corporate Organization

A fundamental rule for the management structure of a QA program is that the Quality Control (QC) function must operate independently from the Manufacturing function.

Quality Control must never report to the Manufacturing function because the conflict of interest is too great. The Manufacturing personnel want to ship the most product at the least cost, and the Quality Control personnel want to ship the highest quality product at whatever the cost. These philosophies are incompatible.

In a small manufacturing company, it is normal and commonplace for the Head of the QA program to report directly to the President of the company. In cases of conflict between QA and Manufacturing, the President shall act as arbitrator, and shall make the final decision.

In larger organizations, the Head of the QA program can report to a Divisional Vice President or a General Manager or Director. In either case, this corporate manager shall act as an impartial arbitrator in cases of conflict.

The Authority and Responsibility of the QA Department

The function of the Head of the QA program is essentially the following:

* To ensure that the QA program and manual is being properly maintained and followed.
* To train and manage the activities of the Quality Control personnel.
* To provide, maintain and calibrate the required testing equipment.
* To maintain records and statistics.
* To maintain certifications of equipment and procedures.
* To represent the company in cases of litigation or disputes arising out of quality complaints.

In cases where the product can impinge directly upon health, safety and well-being, the Head of the QA program is often given the authority to stop production at his or her discretion, if it is believed the product will endanger health or safety. However, this authority is not normally given in companies whose product lines are more mundane.

The QA function is responsible for QC record-keeping. This entails at least the following:

* Determining what quality control records and information to compile and to keep.
* Determining what length of time to keep records.
* Determining what type of quality analyses to perform, e.g. whether to use statistical control techniques or to collect one-shot data.
* Determining what tests to perform.
* Determining what type of testing equipment is required.

* Maintaining a system of product and raw material traceability through record-keeping.

The QA function is also responsible to qualify its QC personnel and all its testing equipment, on a regularly scheduled basis. This entails at least the following:

* To regularly test and qualify QC personnel in the use of the testing equipment.
* To regularly calibrate all testing equipment (i.e. gauges, balances) against a certified standard.
* The issuance and control of inspectors' identification stamps for traceability.
* Maintenance of records of qualification and certification.

A full and complete QA program comprises inspection and record maintenance for incoming raw materials and sub-assemblies, as well as for on-going production, with full traceability of product and raw materials in case of future complaints.

A further responsibility of the QA function, held jointly with the Manufacturing function, is the disposal of non-conforming product. All non-conforming product is normally routed to, and held in, a quarantined area for disposition. The heads of QA and Manufacturing form the core of a Material Review Board (MRB), which decides whether the faulty product can be salvaged and utilized, or whether it must be scrapped. If the product can be salvaged, the QA department assists the Manufacturing department in deciding upon the remedial steps.

The Basic Quality Control System

1. The Quality Assurance Program Manual.

The QA program must have a master manual which details exactly how all aspects of the program will be carried out. It explains who will be responsible for what actions; how to carry out inspections, tests, calibrations, qualifications and certifications; how to file records; how to record for traceability; and in certain cases exactly what inspections and tests to carry out.

The QA manual is the master plan for the program, and it is the responsibility of management to ensure continuous compliance. The most difficult part of starting any QA program is the writing of the QA manual, and assistance from professionals may be required to develop the initial manual.

2. Record-keeping.

It is important that all inspection information, test results, calibration information, specification sheets, certifications and qualifications be recorded and filed for easy access and recall. Lot numbers, batch numbers and incoming material identification numbers must be filed for traceability purposes.

For complex inspections requiring many inputs, for example for the purposes of Statistical Quality Control (SQC), or for the inspection of incoming raw materials, special inspection sheets must be designed by the QA department. The information from these sheets is collected, processed, disseminated and filed in accordance with the requirements of the QA program.

3. Incoming materials inspection.

In order to ensure that the incoming raw materials are not defective, an inspection should be carried out. In certain cases it is necessary to receive certification documents from the supplier, to be able to trace the raw material in case of future quality problems, and to prove the OK status of the raw material.

4. Batches for material control.

Work-in-process is normally separated into identifiable batches, held in bins or on pallets. This is done for two reasons: (i) so that the process of keeping track of the product through the shop is made simpler, and (ii) the traceability of the product in the field is made easier. When there is a flaw revealed by an inspection result, the batch can be isolated from the remainder of the production lot.

It is the responsibility of the Production personnel to keep track of the whereabouts and the status of individual batches.

It is the responsibility of the Shipping department to correctly identify and mark each batch as it leaves the plant.

5. Route sheets for inspection schedules.

The Route sheet is a piece of paper detailing each production step in sequence, that each part in the batch will have to undergo prior to its completion. Every machining operation, i.e. drill, tap, mill, etc. These individual steps may indicate critical dimensions for the operator to remember, or key instructions which may be unusual.

The Route sheet is prepared by the Manufacturing department, is attached to the drawing of the part in question, and is assigned to and identified with a particular batch. If there are two batches of a particular product in the shop, then there will be two identical Route sheets attached to two identical drawings; one for each batch and individually identified.

The Route sheet indicates each required inspection as a production step. For example, if it is necessary to inspect after drill and tap, prior to mill, the Route sheet might read:

Step 7: Drill 3/8"

Step 8: Tap UNF 3/8" 1/2"LG.

** Step 9: Inspect dia. _____ thread. _____ tap lg. _____
    Inspector_____

Step 10: Mill upper face

Each inspection step has a box in which the inspector must indicate OK or HOLD, and a place for the identification number or signature of the inspector.

These Route sheets are collected by the QA department, and stored for recall in case of future problems which may arise at the customer's location, or in the field.

6. The First-off inspection.

In order to eliminate virtually all probability of fault or error, operators are required to ask for an inspection after each new set-up, after completing the operation on only one piece. For example:

Set-up for Drill operation;
Perform the drilling operation on one piece only;

Have the piece inspected;
If OK then drill the remaining pieces in the batch;
If not OK re-do the set-up and repeat the steps.

In this way, a faulty set-up, an incorrect tool or a poorly measured dimension will be picked up immediately, without ruining the entire batch or, worse, the entire lot.

7. Final Inspection.

An inspection of each lot must be carried out prior to packaging, in order to ensure that no errors went undetected during routine inspections in the work-in-process stages. Depending upon the degree of quality and the percent of conformity required by the customer, this final inspection can range from 100% inspection to a simple statistical sampling procedure.

8. Disposition of non-conforming product.

Whenever defective production has been identified, the batch in question must be isolated in a quarantined area, so that it cannot be mistakenly placed back into production. A Material Review Board (MRB) is called to meet and to decide whether the defect can be remedied. If the parts can be salvaged, the remedial action is specified and a special Route sheet is issued for the delinquent batch. If the parts cannot be salvaged, they are scrapped.

A Scrap Report must be issued every time any material is scrapped, and the reason for the rejection clearly stated. The scrap report is generally prepared and issued by the QA department.

Other Important Aspects of the QA Program

1. How often to inspect.

It is important to understand exactly where the vital inspection points are. A program with too many inspection steps is extremely costly, not only because it will require many inspectors, but because each inspection step holds up production while the inspection is being carried out.